WITHDRAWN
HARVARD LIBRARY
WITHDRAWN

Jones, James William, 1943 –

THE REDEMPTION OF MATTER

Towards the Rapprochement of Science and Religion

James W. Jones

UNIVERSITY
PRESS OF
AMERICA

LANHAM • NEW YORK • LONDON

Copyright © 1984 by

University Press of America,™ Inc.

4720 Boston Way
Lanham, MD 20706

3 Henrietta Street
London WC2E 8LU England

All rights reserved
Printed in the United States of America

BL
245
.J66
1984

Library of Congress Cataloging in Publication Data

Jones, James William, 1943–
   The redemption of matter.

   Bibliography: p.
   Includes index.
     1. Religion and science–History of controversy.
I. Title.
BL245.J66   1984   261.5'5   83-21864
ISBN 0–8191–3675–1 (alk. paper)
ISBN 0–8191–3676–X (pbk. : alk. paper)

All University Press of America books are produced on acid-free paper which exceeds the minimum standards set by the National Historical Publications and Records Commission.

FOR SANDY

In him all things were created....Everything was created through him and for him. He is before all things and in him all things hold together. He is the head of the body, the church; he is the origin...that he might be everywhere supreme.
- Paul, **Letter to the Colossians**

Although the whole world is arranged in diverse parts and functions, we must not think it is in a condition of discord and self-contradiction. Just as our one body is composed of many members which are held together by one soul, so I think that the universe ought to be thought of as an immense, complex organism held together by the power and reason of God as by a single soul....God, the Father of all things, fills and holds together the entire cosmos, by his power.
- Origen, **First Principles**

TABLE OF CONTENTS

	Page
INTRODUCTION: BEYOND THE WARFARE OF SCIENCE AND RELIGION	ix
CHAPTER ONE: THE COLLAPSE OF DUALISM	1

Plato 1
Aristotle 3
Stoicism 6
Albinus and Middle Platonism 8
Plotinus and Neo-Platonism 11
The Achievement of Classical Cosmology 16

CHAPTER TWO: THE SACRIFICE OF IMMANENCE 17

Justin Martyr 17
Irenaeus 20
Tertullian 23
Origen 24
The Coming of the Trinity 28

CHAPTER THREE: TOWARDS A MATERIAL SPIRITUALITY 33

Classical Alchemy: Philosophical Background 33
Classical Alchemy: Technical Background 36
The Great Work 39
Alchemy in the Seventeenth Century 45

CHAPTER FOUR: THE RETURN TO DUALISM 49

Mid-Wives to the Machine 49
The Religion of Nature or the Nature
    of Religion 63
The Moral Imperative 67
The Recovery of Presence 70
The Triumph of Separation 74
The Defensive Offensive 79

CHAPTER FIVE: THE DEMISE OF THE MACHINE 82

The Shattering of Matter 82
Immaterialism 85
Complexity 86

TABLE OF CONTENTS (cont.)

	Page
CHAPTER FIVE: THE DEMISE OF THE MACHINE	
Matter and Energy	87
Immaterial Materialism	89
Spirit and Matter	89
Indeterminacy	91
Probability	93
Observing	94
Mechanism and Modern Science	95
Conflict Diminished	96
CHAPTER SIX: THE DIFFUSION OF METAPHYSICS	98
Compartments Sealed	98
After Physics	103
New Light from the East	107
CHAPTER SEVEN: THE BODY OF THE UNIVERSE	115
Towards a Theology of Nature	115
The Immanence and Transcendence Trap	117
Spirit and Matter	118
Freedom	120
Unity	126
The Body of the Universe	131
BIBLIOGRAPHY	134
INDEX	141

INTRODUCTION:

BEYOND THE WARFARE OF SCIENCE AND RELIGION

Part of mankind's perennial pilgrimage of understanding has been the search for a satisfactory comprehension of the physical world. Beginning as a spiritual adventure, other diverse impulses - theological, mathematical, philosophical, pragmatic, and many more - have sought satisfaction throughout its history. This essay begins from the start of this journey, traces its recent division into antagonistic parties called science and religion, and moves from there to suggest how we might travel beyond this dichotomy once again.

The stage is set by those sons of ancient Greece who hammered together the philosophical scenery which forms the backdrop for all ideas that steal across the stage of western history. The next to stand upon the stage are those rightly called the fathers of the church, the beginning of a series of intellectuals who sought to give reasons for the faithful power that dwelt within them by using the most sophisticated rational systems of their day. We are indebted to them not only for the structured forms in which the Christian faith has fruitfully dwelt for almost twenty centuries, but also for the example of their courageous openness to the intellectual currents of an age at least as polymorphously perplexing as our own. From their vocation came forth a theological physics both spiritually profound and philosophically rigorous.

The impulse to understand matter spiritually -- one that rooted itself deeply in the early Christian psyche -- was, however, gradually repressed. The vision lived on in the semi-underground movement of alchemy. Alchemy was always peripheral, carrying as it did the vision of spirit in matter and the power that vision could release, but in this narrative whose theme is recalling that vision and its power, it is right that the alchemists come forward and have a chapter to themselves in which to explain their marriage of divine energy and physical process.

Times changed; that marriage ended in divorce. Men became entranced with a new vision -- the machine -- and peopled the once-lively cosmos with inert levers and wheels busily humming and spinning in purposeless motion. The image of gears and pendulums dominated the human imagination and drove God from the scene. Having tried and failed to take the offensive, theology had no choice but to set up shop somewhere else, walling itself off from the advancing armies of scientific development in dark and airless compartments marked ethics, philosophy, or piety. Thus, the middle section is one long and occasionally bloody battle, ending in God's retreat from the universe he created, and religion's banishment by its one-time ally turned adversary.

In a sense, the first half of the essay is but a prologue to the second. With the fifth chapter, the meat of our drama begins. Christianity modernized itself in the context of this inevitably continuous conflict. Suddenly the scene changes; new characters rush onto the stage; old parts disappear; the script sounds almost like a foreign language, so unfamiliar are its terms and concepts. A new script demands new actors and the stage gradually fills with voices saying that the battle of religion and science can end, the fighting can cease, and the ancient, slumbering Christian dream of experiencing the Spriit in matter and seeing the cosmos as the body of Christ can awaken to consciousness again. Bearing the hope of Christian centuries before the dominance of the machine -- that physical theory might be food for theological reflection -- the final chapter begins again the process of recovering a spiritual vision of matter. The threads binding this essay together are the interactions between religion and science around theories of the physical world, the claim that the dichotomy between religion and science has not always existed and need not exist (at least in its most antagonistic forms) any more and the hope that in moving beyond this antagonism, new theological horizons may open up and old one's be recovered.

As we shall see, in the more integral world of early Christianity the physical cosmos played a crucial role in the theological drama. This book grew out of my search to answer the question of whether the physical world could again be revisioned in a spiritual way. Today, to understand the world, one turns to science. Physics was already something of an avocation with me but I was not prepared for what I found there. After studying generations of bitter conflict between science and religion and coming from a background that compartmentalized them and thus refused to examine the physical world from the perspective of faith, I was astonished at the many ways in which science had changed so much that the older conflict was obsolete. Not only did I realize that the battle between religion and science was no longer necessary, I also saw a rebirth of the ancient dream of physical science enhancing piety. From the womb of physics, new models and images were being born which could be exceptionally fruitful for the spiritual life.

The limited scope of this work must be made clear from the outset. This is not a complete systematic theology to stand proudly beside Aquinas' Summa, Calvin's Institutes, Scheiermacher's Glaubenslehre, or Barth's Dogmatik. It is a much more humble undertaking in which many central Christian beliefs are not covered. Nor is it a popularization of modern physics -- a task far beyond the author's competencies; there is really not much physics here, but those who find what there is perplexing are referred to any of the skillfully-done introductions mentioned in the bibliographical section, and in no sense is this essay considered a substitute for them. Nor is this a general introduction to the interchanges between religion and science. Let the reader beware that many significant areas of concern between them and powerful intellectual movements involving them both are either not mentioned or not done justice. Such general coverage is not necessary, for there are many fine books authored by those more capable than I for such a task. Nor, finally, is this an attempt to resuscitate the honorable eighteenth century tradition of natural theology (in which I do not believe) and to construct a theology out of modern physics. Rather, as a professional scholar of religion, late-comer to physics, and long-time disciple of the spiritual life, my one aim and competency is to help the modern person perceive the material world in a way that enhances the life of faith and to envision it once again as a locus of spiritual power. This work is, however, the down-payment on a new theological enterprise in which the presence and power of the Spirit is again a fundamental and not peripheral category, in which vision returns to its rightful place as the foundation of critical analysis, in which the dominant dichotomies of modernity (especially spirit and matter, religion and science) are passed beyond, and theology is no longer a sectarian intellectual "high" but rather a flame that illumines the cosmos.

Over the many years that this essay has been fashioned and refashioned, I have acquired debts to colleagues so numerous as to require virtually another volume if I were to acknowledge and express individually my gratitude to the various scientists, philosophers, theologians, historians and interested non-specialists who read and made helpful suggests regarding this project as well as to the scores of students whose enthusiasm encouraged me throughout this time. Therefore, this one, general acknowledgment must do for all. In the dedication I have already expressed my deepest sense of gratitude.

J.W.J.
Rutgers University
Summer, 1983

CHAPTER ONE:

THE COLLAPSE OF DUALISM

Plato

Some things pass away; some things are here to stay. In the tumult of time in which we serve out our lives, change is, indeed, the only constant. We plant a seed in the spring; by summer it has disappeared into a flower; by autumn the flower has vanished into the earth. We conceive a son, nurture him in his dependency until, a few short years later, he drives his stubborn will against the limits of our lives, and, a few more years later, he is gone on his own. We give birth to a dream, transform it into a plan which we sow in the cascade of time until it drowns in the current. We read the book of the past: whole nations, peopled with desires, dreams, agonies like our own have arisen, strolled across the landscape, and vanished, while others have come to stand thick upon the stage in their places. The ancients pictured time as a wheel: perpetual motion going nowhere, ceaseless rotation and return.

Some things remain constant. Two stones and two stones heaped together yield four, never five or six. Three lines, when all their tips have been joined, will form a triangle, the sum of whose angles is always one hundred eighty degrees. This is as true in ancient Greece as in Berkeley, California.

From this antithesis of permanance and change, Plato (428 B.C. - 347 B.C.) fashioned a theological cosmology. Around us are things which bombard the senses; they pass away -- no security there. Beyond them the rational mind discovers shapes and mathematical relationships out of which everything is formed; these never change; they are eternal and secure. The world of the senses is transitory and insecure; only a fool would place his hopes there. The world of pure form and number is eternal and wise is the mind that rests in its embrace.

With this distinction, Plato's alter-ego, Timaeus, began the discourse on physics that bears his name. What we see around us is but a reflection of the unchanging world of pure form, shaped by a divine craftsman out of an eternal clay. A workman needs a

1

blueprint and so, gazing upon the ideal world, the transcendent artisan does his best to hammer unruly matter into an edifice most nearly resembling the perfect design from which he works.

The first creative act was thus to impose order on chaos. But such a product was lifeless and static. A second creative act must set it in motion. What causes motion? The motion closest at hand is the movement of our bodies. Where does that arise from? From a principle of life and energy within which Plato calls soul. Thus, Timaeus reasons, if the universe is to be set in motion, it must have a soul. Also, since the creator's goal was to make a work as perfect as possible, and since intelligence is more perfect than stupidity, a stupid cosmos could never approach the perfection of the forms on which it was supposedly patterned. Therefore, the world must be imbued with a rational soul to activate it to move and to insure that its movements will be orderly and reasonably perfect. And so, Timaeus concluded his argument, "The universe came into being as a living creature, endowed with soul and intelligence by the providence of God." Unlike the dead matter which his contemporaries, the atomists, saw as the ultimate structure of the universe, Plato's cosmos was a living organism of body and soul.

Like any organism, the universe has many parts which fit together into a harmonious whole. Each cell of the body is both a living organism in itself and a member of a larger organism. Any organic system has this two-faced quality: Everything that exists is both an individual system and a sub-set of a larger system; all is both a part and a whole, complete and yet partial. To Timaeus, stars, frogs, plants, persons, and all created things are both individual organisms (the stars are referred to as gods, but it is ambiguous whether stones have souls) and limbs of the cosmic animal; stars and people have individual characteristics because of their functions in the universe, but they also participate in the soul of the world.

The divine manufacturer stamps a prefabricated template onto pre-existent material. This is the action of the will. Yet it is not clear how much freedom this cosmic will possesses. Constrained by both the unruliness of matter and the compelling beauty of the good, the heavenly craftsman is more like an automated machine banging out pre-programmed shapes according to a fixed blueprint than a poet selecting the right word from a range of choices. Likewise, the soul of the world, driven by the vision of unchanging beauty, moves the cosmos in a rigid pattern more reminiscent of invariant geometrical shapes than free choice. The world has a soul, and therefore, an immanent will; but it's not clear whether this will contains the ability to choose.

To human beings, the rational soul supplies life and intelligence. Through reason, a person can discover transcendental mathematical relations, compose harmonious music, speculate on universal laws. Here the finite and transitory limits of the body are transcended, the eternal touched. The soul may indwell a finite body, but its affinity is for the eternal. Plato remained enticingly obscure about the relations among all these transcendent entities -- ideas, souls, gods -- but the basic point is clear: The human soul spans the daily drudgery of the finite earth and the splendors of the eternal kingdom. Likewise, with the soul of the world, it animates and orders the cosmos from within but ultimately belongs to the eternal world beyond.

Aristotle

When Plato died in 347 B.C., his former pupil Aristotle (384 B.C. - 322 B.C.) departed the Academy and struck out on his own. More empirical than rational, he left Plato's heavenly mathematics to lose himself in the multiplicity of earthly creatures. A biologist more than a geometer, Aristotle discovered that living organisms could not be understood abstractly like triangles and cubes. Eternal, unchanging shapes shed no light on the varigated flux of plant and animal development. There is in Aristotle a driving polemic against the Platonic idea of the forms -- it is the power of the dynamic against the static, the revolt of the particular against the universal. Vitality and change cannot be encompassed by rigid and invariant structures; a shifting kaleidoscope cannot be grasped through the lens of universal forms.

Rather than form, function is most important for understanding living systems. From his empirical labors, Aristotle details his four famous causes.

Obviously not causes in the modern sense (Toulmin and Goodfield call them the four "be-causes"), they are really four fundamental answers to the question, "Why?". They are:

1. The material -- from what is it made?

2. The formal -- what essence or form does it take?

3. The precipitant -- by what act did it happen?

4. The teleological -- to what goal is it directed?

Understanding an event or organism totally means viewing it in this multi-modal way. If I have cut down a tree and someone asks why it fell, I can answer:

1. Materially -- It was made of wood, a "sawable" substance.

2. Formally -- It was maleable and strong, and, therefore, suited to build a house.

3. Precipitantly -- It was cut by a substance harder and sharper than itself; i.e., a metal saw.

4. Teleologically -- I wanted to build a house.

Function clearly implies purpose; the first three causes are held together by the fourth. Aristotle's science is unashamedly teleological.

Empirical investigation, for Aristotle, begins and ends with direct apprehension of the physical world; his science is more description than theory. Needing no reference beyond the given and sensible -- his four causes belong wholly to this world -- he has no use for Plato's crucial distinction between this world and the eternal one. Aristotle's universe is autonomous, self-contained, comprehensible on its own terms alone. As acutely conscious as Plato of movement and change within the world, Aristotle feels no need to explain it. Nature is inherently dynamic, possessing an innate impulse to motion. Aristotle, true to his temperament, refuses to speculate on any immanent source of all this activity other than the

order of nature itself. There is no world soul, no
elan vital. While God is not anthropomorphized,
nature is. Aristotle speaks of nature as "acting like
a good housekeeper who throws away nothing that is
useful" and who "does nothing vain or unnecessary".
The thrifty and efficient cosmos is its own cause.
Whereas for Plato, the cosmos adds nothing to an
all-sufficient God, for Aristotle God adds nothing to
an all-sufficient cosmos.

This does not, however, mean that there is no
place for God. The heavenly rotation, so perfectly
circular to Aristotle's eyes, could not be accidental.
Such motion demands a mover. Since it would be the
source of all motion, Aristotle reasons, it can have
no source but itself -- it is an unmoved mover. The
only motion which is the source of itself is
self-contemplation. Totally and completely
self-sufficient, God lives in glorious autonomy,
contemplating his own beauty. Such a God cannot move
the cosmos directly. Rather, the cosmos, too,
attracted by the divine beauty, moves in contemplation
of God's splendor. God moves the heavens as a distant
object of attention, not as an immanent cause.
Attending to nothing but himself, Aristotle's deity
sits and looks beautiful while the heavens spin
around, literally in circles, trying to capture his
beauty.

If the universe is moved by contemplation, it
must have a mind of its own, and so Aristotle endowed
the stars and planets with intelligence by which they,
like human beings, seek after God and so are set in
motion. But he does not propose, as Plato did, the
idea of a mind immanent in the universe. For
Aristotle, there is no separate and subsisting soul,
no realm of ideas from which to come or to which to
return. Human life is but a system of coordinated
functions. The cosmos, too, lacks soul and is but a
pattern of autonomous movements.

While Aristotle saw continuity between plant,
animal, and human life, arranging them on a
hierarchical scale from stones to philosophers, and
envisioned a teleology in nature, there is no doctrine
of progressive evolution in Aristotle. Nor is there
any hint that God or divinization is the goal of
cosmic motion. The divine remains forever distant
from the world; the motion God inspires is not a

progressive ascent but an endless, repetitive circularity.

Stoicism

While Stoicism is a movement whose roots are lost in the Aegean mists of antiquity, its fruit blossomed with the flowering of the Graeco-Roman world. Like Timaeus' narrative, Stoicism reveals the impulse towards a theological physics. Many Stoic themes echo the mythmaker from Italy: The cosmos is a great animal born from the marriage of two principles -- the spiritual and the material; spirit is active and intelligent, matter is passive and dumb. Like Timaeus' cosmos, the Stoic's universe is composed of sub-systems organized into an organic whole. As opposed to Aristotle's reductionism, the Stoic's organic cosmos is more than the sum of its parts. Its systemic properties arise from the pneuma or breath incarnate in the universe. Such a breath or spirit (the word "pneuma" means both in Greek) cannot be directly observed but is known by its effects, especially the order and coordination of the universe. Pneuma pervades the cosmos, holding it together, powering its motion, governing all events. Religiously inclined Stoics called it god, or Zeus; those philosophically inclined called it fate or reason; the most common Greek philosophical term for it was "logos".

There is much here reminiscent of Plato, but it is Plato with a strikingly non-Platonic twist. While asserting a dualism of soul and body, spirit and matter, Stoics were thorough-going materialists. Soul and body were both physical substances. Pneuma was not, a'la Plato, pure intelligence or spirit but rather very finely ground matter. Rather than separate orders of being, the cosmos is a system of increasingly coarse particles. Not a discrete entity, the soul is diffused through the body like sand mixed with pebbles on the beach. While accepting Plato's argument for the existence of a soul, Stoics agreed with Aristotle that it is not a separate mode of being.

Thus, the theology spun out of the physics is radically different from Plato's. There is no transcendent world of ideas; the goal of life is not the release of the soul from the prison of matter or its escape through contemplation to a higher realm. There is no God apart from the universe -- not the creative artisan of the Timaeus, not the ideal fountainhead of goodness hinted at in the Republic, not the gloriously distant unmoved mover of the Metaphysics. The only God is the immanent logos, the organizing principle of the world which rules and determines all events. Resignation to this immanent determinism is the secret of blessedness. Union with God is not an escape from the flux of the world, but an interior conformity of heart and will to the mind of this all-governing spirit. Salvation is the peace that comes from accepting everything as the will of God; theology is physics conducted with reverence.

Likewise, the physics is different from anything Plato or Aristotle would call science. The Stoic world, too, is totally autonomous; it needs no external act of will to stamp it into order; rather, it grows out of the seed of life within it. But the autonomy of nature and a consistent materialism are not pitted against the existence of a world soul but, rather, are made to serve it. The world soul is precisely what makes nature autonomous; it is the life principle in the living animal of the cosmos. Not a half-way being between the creator and the world like Timaeus' immanent soul, the logos is the piece the classical world found missing from Aristotle's metaphysical puzzle; it explains what Aristotle himself felt no need to explain -- the dynamic of nature. But there is no reason to multiply entities needlessly; if earthly motion can be accounted for by an immanent causation, so also with the motion of the heavens. Aristotle's narcissistic mover is superfluous. There is no transcendent deity in Stoicism. Plants grow, men run, stars rotate, just as blood circulates -- all are the motions of life within the living universe.

A system of tremendous simplicity and coherence, morality and cosmology are rolled into one. Perennial questions of the nature of the cosmos, its origin, motion, and life are answered by reference to one pervasive pneuma. The character of the good life which occupied Socrates and his "yes-men" for days is captured by a single image -- "apathea" -- or resignation to the inevitable ordering of the same pervading power. No system offered its adherents more serenity or elegance.

Albinus and Middle Platonism

The major cities of the Graeco-Roman era -- Athens, Corinth, Rome, Alexandria -- would rival Berkeley, Harvard Square, Manhattan, London, or Tokyo as melting-pots or boiling cauldrons of ideologies and life-styles. The intellectual stews simmering in Athens or Alexandria freely blended Platonism, Stoicism, Aristotelianism, and many others. The rank empiricism of Aristotle never captured the mind of the ancient world, even while his ideas were borrowed freely. His descriptive inclination would have to wait for other times and places to be appreciated. Plato was the master, even though his ideas were distorted almost beyond recognition. A favorite intellectual pastime seems to have been creating commentaries on Plato, attributing to him popular ideas which he clearly repudiated. One such commentary is the tract, attributed to one Albinus, called the <u>Didaskalikos</u> or the "Epitome of the Teachings of Plato", representing a Platonism mid-way between the Socratic dialogues and the new Platonism of Plotinus.

Origin was the primary theo-physical question on Albinus' mind -- How did the cosmos begin? --as opposed to Plato's focusing on its form and Aristotle its function. According to Albinus, there are three "originals", three "beginnings", which are the same as those found in the <u>Timaeus</u>: the ideas, the creator, and matter. These are the three "firsts" <u>(archae</u> in Greek); no account of their origin is possible; they are just given, the first principles from which everything else derives. There is also Plato's dualism, rescued from the materialistic monism of the Stoics, of two orders of being: the uncreated reality, stable and eternal, and the created order, transitory and temporal. The second depends on the first, not for its existence, since matter is one of the eternals, but for its organization. This much is plagiarism from the <u>Timaeus</u>.

The cosmology is similar, the theology is different. For Albinus, the ideas from which the world is duplicated are not an independent realm but are thoughts in the mind of God. A stroke of redefinition transforms the theology of Plato (Philo of Alexandria -- a Jewish middle-Platonist -- made the same move). God is now a supreme being of intellectual self-sufficiency, more of an Aristotelian image than a Platonic one. Timaeus' god was a slave of the eternal forms, a manipulator of plans but not an original thinker. By making the blue-print of the cosmos a thought conceived by God, the world literally becomes God's idea. Reversing Plato's hierarchy, the forms are now dependent upon God. Albinus approaches the image of a transcendent creator, not in the Judeo-Christian sense of an originator out of nothing, but certainly one far more potent than the artisan of the Timaeus. More than a midrash on Plato, the <u>Didaskalikos</u> has syncretized three popular images: Timaeus' craftsman, Plato's transcendent idea of the good as the source of all ideas, Aristotle's prime mover.

Albinus' god is set totally beyond the finite world. God comprehends all, and is therefore incomprehensible; God is one and whole, the world is fragmentary and incomplete; God is forever going beyond; the world is forever limited. No finite, particular, limited image can apply to one who is beyond even being itself. Albinus writes: "The primary God is eternal, ineffable, complete in itself; that is, not wanting anything, ever complete; that is, forever complete, all sufficient, complete in every way." In this deft combination of the maker, the model, and the source from Plato with the Aristotelian image of the unmoved mover, however, Albinus fails to notice that the Platonic and Aristotelian images refer to different models of transcendence. As Plotinus would discover, a Platonic amalgamation of maker, model, and source yields a transcendental fountain of existence beyond all <u>knowledge</u>, <u>epistemically</u> transcending the finite world; but as the origin of all, this God is the first in a unified <u>hierarchy of being</u> radiating out from it. Not <u>ontologically</u> transcendent to the finite world, God is, rather, bound to the world as its source. Aristotle's unmoved mover is in precisely the opposite position. As rationally necessary to explain the cause of motion, Aristotle's God is easily comprehensible, but he has no connection with the physical world, dwelling in total separation from it. When the church fathers took over the framework of middle Platonism, their inability to differentiate these two models of transcendence created puzzles enough to occupy generations of theologians.

Giving Timaeus' humble and hardworking manufacturer the exalted, if isolated, status of

Aristotle's unmoved mover creates an obvious problem -- how can such an uninvolved figure produce something? No artisan can work at such a distance from his subject. To answer this, Albinus refurbishes the Platonic schema of a world soul. What was a minor plank, however, becomes a central pillar. Thrown in almost as an afterthought, Timaeus' world soul is there to account for motion (one of creation's less desirable features) and to make up for matter's lack of intelligence. To the author of the Didaskalikos, the soul of the world is more than just another soul; it is a second God -- creative and eternal in its own right. The supreme deity is so transcendent, unmoved and self-sufficient that the world soul must fill the void between the high deity and the cosmos, becoming a mediator and co-creator in its own right.

The mediating world soul is not, as in Plato, inserted into matter by God, but is eternally incarnate in the stuff of the universe. Matter has always possessed a soul; it has never been totally dumb or lifeless. Albinus made the Stoic's eternal logos perform the expanded functions of Plato's world soul, allying spirit and matter more closely than Plato would have dared. The world soul, Albinus wrote, lay asleep many eons but was graciously awakened by the beauty of the supreme being. Shaking off its drowsiness, the world soul began to turn towards the high God and bask in his radiance. Beholding and reflecting the divine beauty the logos gradually took on the attributes of the transcendent deity and, in doing so, stabilized and harmonized the unruly matter of which it is the heart. Aristotle's theory of the action over distance by which the world turns is joined with Plato's vision of the soul's transformation through contemplation, so that aesthetics becomes the key to cosmology. Plato's primal dualism of two realities becomes a theological dualism of two gods -- one of Aristotelian transcendence, and one of Stoic immanence -- whom Christian theology would struggle for centuries to combine into one.

The primal problem of origin is solved by an artful combination of Platonism, Stoicism, and Aristotelianism; the result is a schema of poetic beauty and theological complexity. The security and conceptual purity of transcendence is combined with the immediacy of immanence. The scientifically simple Stoic explanation of the dynamic order of nature is fused with powerful mythic imagery worthy of Timaeus himself. The essential religious act for the soul of man, as for the soul of the world, is transformation by contemplation. Such was the intellectual coinage given to the fathers of the Christian church in which to transact their business.

Plotinus and Neo-Platonism

The transcendental sensibilities of Plato continued to hold more fascination for the classical world than the empirical mindset of Aristotle. Lacking self-sufficiency, nature points beyond itself to a divine source; incomplete on its own terms, physics must find its fulfillment in theology. This impulse towards trandscendence climaxes in Plotinus (205-270 A.D.), a contemporary of the third century fathers of Christian Platonism, Clement and Origen.

In the Republic, Plato had spoken of the "Form of the Good" which shines through the rest of the Forms, illuminating all objects of knowledge as the sun illuminates the physical world. As the sun is the source of both the colors which we see and the light by which we see them, but is not the colors or the sightings themselves, so the "Form of the Good" is beyond all the forms. The "Form of the Good" transcends even being itself and so is more exalted than both the forms of particular objects and the objects themselves for it is the source of both. Also, in the Symposium, Plato had suggested the vision of the "Supreme Beauty" or the "Supreme Good" is the goal of the philosophic journey. Although this exalted "Form of the Good" plays relatively little role in Plato's philosophizing, it became increasingly important to his successors. The image of a hierarchy of being extending up from the physical world through the world of forms to culminate in a supreme and transcendental source which is an object of contemplation become central to Plotinus' schema and to later, medieval, Christian mysticism.

Plato's cosmology had three "originals" -- the form, the former, and the formed; the idea of a supreme form was ancillary to the general theory of forms. The second member of this trinity became increasingly pre-eminent. In middle-Platonism, the trinity was, for all practical purposes, reduced to a duality. The supreme God, or former of the universe, predominates; he is now the source of the form of the world and its fashioner rolled into one. As the source of the forms, he takes over the transcendent glory of Plato's "Form of the Good". Over-against the high God lay the sombulent but equally eternal matter. In Plotinus, the reduction of trinity to duality is taken the next step and becomes a consistent monism.

In Plotinus, there is but a single first principle -- the ONE, the only arche, the source beyond all being. As the fountain of all existence, it does not itself exist for it is bound to no categories, not even the notion of existence or being. To exist, for Plotinus, is to be thrown into particularity and contingency, to be transitory, eventually to pass away. Thus, transcendence pushes over the brink of finite intelligibility.

To Plato, Aristotle, the Stoics, and even the author of the Didaskolilkos, human intelligence could form some analogue to the divine -- it was like an artisan, or a mind engulfed in beauty, or a finely spun substance, or a transcendent object contemplation. To Plotinus, no such analogy is possible -- the ONE is beyond time and space and no categories drawn from the three-dimensional world apply.

The ONE of which Plotinus speaks is not the first in a sequence of similar numbers but is rather ONE in the sense of a unity. The three-dimensional world is the realm of fragments; the ONE is an undifferentiated whole which, because of its oneness, is universal, pervasive, inclusive of all things. As Plato's idea of the good encompasses the individual ideas, Plotinus' ONE is the source of all particular entities in the cosmos. The ONE contains the many.

Such a ONE is not, however, static. Containing all that is, it fulfills itself by turning itself inside out, projecting outward all that is within. Creation is not the product of the willful act of an artisan, nor a response to a distant and unmoved mover, nor the immanent energy of a world soul, but rather, the overflow of a cosmic well. The image of a fountain gushing forth more captures the Plotinian meaning than that of an artisan carving his work or blood pulsating through the veins. Matter is not the product of selection from among alternatives but of an impulse to emanation and diffusion, as the sun shines or radium gives off radioactivity.

The cosmos exists first as an idea in the mind of the ONE -- a theory similar to that of the Didaskolilkos -- but an idea endowed with its own impulse towards materialization and pushing outward into existence. The ONE is a repository of forms driven by the blind compulsion towards self-expression. Every form must be manifest and thus everything exists of necessity to fulfill the plenitude of being. No fault can be found with creation for all is required to complete the self-manifestation of the source. The highest good is not the morality of decision but, rather, the state of wholeness or completion. To be perfect is not to conform of some external law but to be completely fulfilled. The cosmos is perfect; everything is necessary to the cosmic continuity; nothing is superfluous or lacking; the cosmos is full and whole.

The ONE becomes the many by a series of radiations or emanations. First to be radiated is MIND -- this is the supreme God of Middle-Platonism, the model and the manufacturer of the Timaeus combined. This is the God to whom religion looks; not the first principle, God himself has a source in one more primal. MIND, in turn, generates SOUL, who pervades all things; this is both the animating world-soul of Stoicism and Middle-Platonism and the individual contemplative soul of Plato. Immaterial and immortal, SOUL diffuses everywhere: imposing order on all things, governing their activities, giving them life. Having come out, MIND and SOUL turn from this centrifugal expulsion from the divine abyss and return to it in contemplation. To Plotinus, the cosmos is a vast, pulsating organism, continually being radiated from its source, and continually being reunited with it by contemplative unification.

Plotinus' system reveals the same impulse as that of his universe -- the drive towards synthesis. Bringing together the loose strands of ancient philosophy, made popular by a kind of religio-philosophical natural selection, Plotinus weaves them into a seamless robe in which all dualism and dichotomies are lost in the ONE. Where others saw separate entities or modes of being, Plotinus sees only the continuous expression of a common source in which all exist first as archetypes. What is self-contained is neither the empirical world or the transcendent God but, rather, the single, continuously flowing and pulsating process of self-expression that generates them both.

Spirit is the source of matter but spirit and matter are the opposite ends of the cosmic continuum: Spirit is the most powerful, matter the most inert; spirit the most substantial, matter the least. At the opposite end of the cosmic scale, matter is spirit shading off into non-existence; it is almost illusory. Matter is poverty of spirit. The Source is pure spirit, with no trace of matter; it is epistemically beyond the knowledge of those darkened by the shadow of materiality. Pure spirit is not, however, a separate order of being, for the material universe is the furthest frontier of the continuous reach of the spirit. In this reverse Stoicism, matter is seen as increasingly rarified spirit.

The soul, too, at least at its center, is beyond space and time, possessing the possibility of union with the ONE. All the hypostases of God inhere in the soul. Contemplation is the soul's realization of this oneness -- all boundaries are shed, multiplicity vanishes, the soul merges again with its source, or meets its source in itself. On its way from the eternal realm to becoming embodied, the soul has passed through several celestial realms -- spiritual, astral, ethereal, and finally, physical -- such was the teaching of Plato. By introspection, the soul passes through analogous levels within itself to reach its immanent but transcendental source. The metaphysical entities existing within the cosmic hierarchy are also, for Plotinus, states of consciousness. Consciousness is the primary reality, the key to understanding spirit and therefore, matter. Consciousness unlocks the secret of cosmology after all spatial and material language has been shed (the terms immanence and transcendence are used for lack of others; they are really anachronistic and meaningless in this context). Spirit is the essence of matter; psyche the heart of soma. Thus Plotinus said, the body is in the soul, not the soul in the body. The ONE is the largest, most substantial, reality; it enfolds the universe within itself while being diffused throughout the system. The soul contains the world, and so through consciousness of the soul, the world is comprehended.

In most classical (or at least post-Platonic) philosophy, matter is the surd; no satisfactory answer to the question of its raison d'etre was ever given. Plato used matter to explain the soul's distraction from the ideal. To gnostic contemporaries of Plotinus and others like Numenius of Apamea, matter is unremittingly evil; Numenius insisted that matter is totally independent of divine control. Albinus, while calling matter created, could not give up the Platonic-Aristotelian insistence on its eternity and with his usual ingenuity solved the problem of making matter both created and eternal by making it eternally generated. Matter, and the world Soul that vivifies it, become subsidiary eternal principles. Plotinus took the trend towards the subordination of matter to its inescapable conclusion, making matter totally dependent on a transcendent source; it is simply an emanation, and not an eternal principle at all.

Albinus' notion of eternal generation moderated the Platonic opposition between an eternal, uncreated realm and a transitory, created one, but it made little sense in that dualistic framework. Plotinus' theory of emanation gives the term eternal generation a consistent meaning for the first time; in doing so, he undercut the Platonic antagonism of spirit and matter. Plotinus was true to Plato in regarding matter as the locus of evil, but what makes matter suspect is not the lure of its distractions or its inherent impulse towards disorder, but rather its utter lack of power and the illusion of its substantiality. Plotinus did what Plato and the gnostics were unable to do: give matter a negative connotation while still insisting it was created by God. What is lost is the dualistic idea of matter as an independent principle of evil -- an idea that reached its culmination in the systems of Numenious, Valentinus, and the gnostics -- an undeniably Platonic image that finds no place in Plotinus.

Plotinus devised a coherent alternative to the religions of his day, complete with mystical experience, theodicy, and ethics. He vehemently rejected all cults, redeemers, schemes of salvation. His mysticism requires transformation by meditation through which the soul returns to its source in a dazzling moment of self-realization. The cosmos is its own explanation; arising from a source beyond change and multiplicity, which spreads out, creating a hierarchy of increasingly material beings, until the most intelligent of them reverse the process, and, by sheer intellectual vigor, regain their origin. With all dualisms overcome, the Platonic impulse towards simplicity and transcendence finds its fulfillment in Plotinus; the ultimate elegance which Plato sought in geometry, Plotinus found in mysticism.

The Achievement of Classical Cosmology

All classial cosmologists agreed that origin provides the clue to nature; to understand the cosmos meant to tell a story about its beginning. Telling this story is the task of a unified intellectual endeavor which the modern age has divided in two (into physics and theology, which have been further subdivided into such things as astrophysics, high-energy physics, apologetics, and ethics). The reason for telling the story was not abstract and empirical but personal and moral: to answer the primal questions of the nature of things, the reality of God, and the principles of moral conduct. Classical cosmology spoke to all these human longings with a single theory. Conversely, understanding the cosmos was a religious and moral imperative; not that it was a duty, but through struggling to comprehend the universe, God was found, the good life discovered, and moral and spiritual growth took place.

Plato passed along a set of ideas that culminated in the cosmologies of Middle and Neo-Platonism which mitigated the rigid dualism which was, for him, the key to reality. Spirit and matter were brought closer together as the theory of the world-soul (peripheral in Plato) became increasingly prominent. Instead of being an evil impediment to spiritual growth, the world came to be seen as animated and indwelt by an immanent spiritual presence. Rather than being the product of a semi-divine craftsman and a recalcitrant substance, creation was later perceived as the direct emanation of divine beneficence. Rather than an appendage to be discarded as quickly as possible, the physical order was said to have a spiritual destiny of its own. Neither Albinus or Plotinus would go as far as the Christian confession of faith and call creation "good", but both of them saw a sacramental marriage of spirit and matter, where Plato could only see a divorce.

CHAPTER TWO:

THE SACRIFICE OF IMMANENCE:

Justin Martyr

Some find their God in face-to-face encounters, rather than in ascending ecstasies of intuition; they seek a personal center of intelligence and volition behind the physical world. Such were the ancient Hebrews who bequeathed to the infant Christian community their sacred scriptures which open with the words, "In the beginning God created the heavens and the earth." The impulse behind these words was to set a divine creative will over-against a dependent world. This forced the fathers of the church to begin an unceasing theological tradition of struggling to harmonize sacred text and scientific theory. On the surface, it seems apparent that Genesis pictures a God set apart from creation and simultaneously, the source of its being. For Justin Martyr (100 - 165 A.D.), among the first in what would become a long line of secular philosophers converted to the gospel of Jesus, these two images -- God's transcendence and the world's dependence -- must be preserved, but they must also be understood in terms of the accepted truth about the cosmos fashioned by Plato and updated by the eclectic teachers of middle-Platonic era.

The transcendence of God seemed the easier problem. The middle-Plotonic amalgamation of Platonic and Aristotelian notions into an ineffable and self-sufficient being provided Justin with precisely the image of God that he required. Thus, Justin continually spoke of God in words that Albinus would have appreciated: "uncreated", "ineffable", "nameless", and "unmoved". These terms, used in the context of Plato's primal dualism of two orders of reality, enabled Justin to carry out the basic theological task as he understood it -- setting God apart from the world. For Justin, God's primary attribute is his immutability; God is the sole uncreated, the one occupant of Plato's realm of being. This explains Justin's uncompromising vehemence against pagan polytheism. Whereas, for Plato the eternal realm contained many inhabitants -- gods, souls, spirits, etc., for Justin it held only one: the supreme God. All else was created. Hence, a problem Justin did not notice when he conceived of God's transcendence in terms of Plato's rigid distinction, growing daily less rigid among Justin's non-Christian colleagues. Plato's dichotomy implies opposition: to call God eternal and immutable is to say more than just that God is unknowable or imcomprehensible; it is to set God in opposition to the finite world of temporality and change.

This brought Justin into conflict with another tenet of the evolving Christian faith -- that God is related to the world as creator and governor. Did not Jesus say that God loves the world? But how can the eternal love the transitory when they represent two worlds that are on Plato's terms, morally and ontologically irreconcilable? To answer this, Justin had recourse to another middle-Platonic image -- the logos or world-soul. Justin, like Albinus, used the Stoic idea of the logos in a transformed way. The materialism of the early Stoics was anathema to the fathers of eastern Christianity but by the time of Justin, middle-Platonists like Albinus had incorporated the logos within a Platonic framework by identifying it with Timaeus' world-soul. Now the logos is immaterial spirit, not material substance. This redefinition of the logos made it safe for Christian use.

Already, within the New Testament, the gospel of John had begun the process of describing Jesus in philosophical language. John opens with the magnificent equation of Jesus with the logos - "In the beginning was the word (logos)....and the word (logos) became flesh and dwelt among us" - and the theology of the fathers, centering on the image of the logos, can be seen as a logical development from this gospel. With John's gospel in hand, it is natural that Justin would use the same term -- now given a middle-Platonic meaning -- to describe the role of Christ. The functions of Christ become the functions of the world-soul: Christ represents both the immanence of God in the cosmos and the mediator between the Transcendent and the world. Christ is the seed of truth sown throughout the world; the power of God residing within the universe. The identification of Jesus with the world-soul deftly explains Christ's role in a way comprehensible to the people of Justin's day, but this explanation in the context of Middle-Platonism which had solved the problem of divine transcendence and immanence by having two Gods, led to a further question - how is Christ the Son of God? The attempts to answer this question would, in turn, produce, the doctrine of the Trinity. In fighting over how to relate the Son to the Father, the logos to the high God, the fathers were struggling over God's relation to creation, and their solution would have profound effects on the place of cosmology in theology.

To explicate the transcendence of God, Justin drew on Plato's rigid dichotomy of two orders of reality: To explicate the role of Christ he used middle-Platonism's image of the world-soul which evolved precisely to break down that rigid dichotomy. Put most sharply, his dilemma was -- Where does the logos belong? Is it created or uncreated? If God is the sole uncreated, the world is obviously created; it belongs to the realm of becoming, change, flux, and finitude. Bridging this chasm is the logos through whom, according to John's gospel, God created the world. In middle-Platonism the logos does not create out of nothing but rather brings order into a disordered matter. Thus Justin did not advocate creation <u>ex nihilio</u>; his favorite image for God was Timaeus' craftsman who shapes the formless substance that existed eternally. The world is not eternal; it is dependent and transitory, and had a beginning in time. Justin said, however, that the term "world" in the scriptures refers to the cosmos as a rationally ordered system. This smoothly functioning universe began in time and is dependent upon God. It exists as <u>cosmos</u> by virtue of the ordering logos within. However it did not come into being out of nothing but was, rather, "formed" and "molded" from chaotic matter into an organization of beauty.

What, then, of the logos through whom the world is shaped? Platonism, with its propensity for the plural, had many uncreated beings -- souls, the artisan, the forms, and later, the world-soul of Albinus; Justin's Judeo-Christian monotheism allows only one, the supreme God. Justin's use of the logos as mediator and co-creator implies that he belongs to both orders simultaneously, which makes little sense in light of the chasm separating them. Justin could not say the Son was uncreated for the glory of the Father gave that status tò him alone; Justin could not say the son was created, for how could he be called Lord? His solution was to call the son both created and divine. The Logos-Son is created, but in a different way: He is the "first generate", the "only begotten" or "first begotten", the "divinely generated" -- a creature who is somehow divine. Justin rehabilitated Plato's radical dualism in order to preserve the transcendent uniqueness of God, but then found that he had to mitigate it in precisely the same direction as middle-Platonism in order to explain the role of the mediator between the supreme being and the world.

Teaching God's transcendence by calling him the sole ungenerated gives new meaning to old terms. Now the primary distinction between the orders of being and becoming is that one, God, is independent, while the other, the world, is dependent. Creation refers to the universe's mode of being, not to its having had an absolute beginning in time. Justin went to his martyrdom content that he had preserved the Christian faith by making the cosmos dependent -- a living organism sustained by its life-giving and harmonizing interior spirit -- even though it was not born from nothing.

Irenaeus

Shortly after Justin earned his sobriquet in the arena presided over by the Stoic emperor Marcus Aurelius, his former pupil Irenaeus (whose life spanned the second half of the second century) became bishop of Gaul. While Justin had been a philosopher convert, Irenaeus was a prince and soldier of the church defending the faith of his childhood. Most of Justin's writings were directed towards the world; most of Irenaeus' were directed to believers to make them more secure. Justin sought to convert others, like himself, born outside the church; Irenaeus sought to rid his ancestral faith of enemies within. The enemies Irenaeus particularly had in mind were the gnostics. While the tortured history of gnosticism is far beyond our scope, it is clear Irenaeus' adversaries maintained two aspects of Platonism most antithetical to the developing Christian faith: a propensity for pluralism and the evilness of the material. Starkly dualistic, these second century gnostics inhabited two contrary worlds: the pleroma, which contained a host of spiritual beings, and the physical world, created and controlled by impulses contradictory to the spirit. Through secret initiation, <u>gnostikoi</u> learned about shedding matter and returning to the pleroma. Gnosticism represents Plato's dualism religiously carried to its furthest extreme.

Irenaeus found in Justin's adaptations of middle-Platonism exactly the weapons needed to defeat gnosticism. To the vision of a pleroma of eternal spirits, Irenaeus opposed Justin's doctrine of the sole, uncreated God. The radical monotheism of Justin entailed that all other beings -- souls, spirits, angels, and demons -- the whole cast of the gnostic drama of redemption -- were all creatures of the one divine father and not eternal powers in their own right. Justin's distant and transcendent God was the perfect antidote to an eternal community of spirits, and Irenaeus embraced it gladly.

Such a totally transcendent deity, however, played into another part of the gnostic system -- its dualism. Justin's theology of transcendence and the gnostic myth of redemption both drew on Plato's irreconcilable dualism of the temporary and the eternal. As a hedge against gnosticism, Irenaeus had to embrace the doctrine of transcendence without the corollary of an unbridgeable chasm between God and the world. He did this by emphasizing the limitlessness of God. God contains all things, encompasses all things, and all things participate in him. The pleroma is God himself: the immeasurable matrix of being, in which the whole world is contained. Whereas Justin's model of transcendence stresses the "apartness" of God from the world, Irenaeus' image points to the intimate relationship of God with every aspect of creation, opposing the gnostic doctrine of irreconcilability. Of course, there is an implication which Irenaeus never noticed -- If God is without boundaries, what keeps all particulars from eventually being consumed by the divine source? Are not all creatures destined to be swallwed up in the limitless ocean of being which is God?

Another gnostic teaching to which Justin's theology provided a ready rebuttal was the evilness of matter. Rather than being estranged from God, Irenaeus said, matter is indwelt by the divine logos which is "united and mingled with his own creation". Justin's Logos, modeled after the middle-Platonic world-soul who is "through all things" is the intellectual cure for the gnostic poison of hostility between spirit and matter. The physical cannot be evil, for it is born from spirit.

This, however, generates anoher problem: Justin needed a mediator because he emphasized divine distance; Irenaeus' doctrine of transcendence as omnipresence already binds God and world together; why, then, the logos? Not needing the logos as mediator, Irenaeus' focus falls on the logos as immanent presence; the logos "in an invisible way contains everything which has been made and is immanent in the whole creation for the Word of God guides and arranges all things." Justin, following Albinus, implied that the logos was sort of "half-way" between the deity and creation, but to Irenaeus, such semi-divine beings smell of gnosticism. Thus, he pushed harder than Justin on the quivalence of God and the logos. Whereas Justine clearly describes Christ as a second-order divinity, Irenaeus insists that Jesus is co-eternal and co-existent with God, playing down Justin's claim that the logos is generate.

For Irenaeus, no less than Justin, to invoke the logos is to become involved with cosmology. Unfortunately, the middle-Platonic idea of the world-soul inherent in matter and the eternally subsisting logos of John's gospel -- both of which Irenaeus was heir to -- are drawn from different cosmologies. In middle-Platonic terms, the logos is intimately tied up with creation rather than being a part of the deity. Irenaeus used the logos in its middle-Platonic sense of one indwelling and ordering creation. However, since the logos is eternal, this function must be eternal. Middle-Platonism could not separate the logos from the world; Irenaeus could not separate the logos from God, and so ended up implying that the world, too, is eternally generated. "The Father," he said, "sustains the creation and his logos at the same time." The logos is less of a go-between and more of an indwelling source. Thus, Irenaeus can argue against the gnostics that creation is good because the divine logos inheres within it but the price paid for this argument in middle-Platonic logic is the implication that creation is eternal.

In rejecting gnosticism, Irenaeus was driven beyond Justin in another area: Irenaeus decisively breaks with the Platonic image of God as an artisan shaping a resistant medium, asserting once and for all that creation is out of nothing. The only force in the universe is God's creative power which brings all things into being "out of that which had no existence". God is primarily being, the source of being who "grants to all things their very existence". The cosmos is not set in opposition to God, nor seen as an autonomous system independent of his sovereignty, rather, it is an expression of his eternally overflowing being, the externalization of his eternally creative will.

In opposing the gnostics, Irenaeus moved beyond Justin's multi-leveled cosmology of a transcendent God, a mediating logos, and a dependent world to a more unified system in which God transcends and yet is also, paradoxically, bound up with the world. Matter is a manifestation of his endlessly creative volition, the physical face of the spiritually omnipresent, divine logos.

Tertullian

The Christian community grew to maturity in an environment unmatched for its diversity and pluralism. Within Platonism, and the same was true of the other schools of ancient Greece, ideas tended to diffuse, dissipate, and recombine in a cacophony of conflicting street-corner expositors. The predominate impulse in Christianity was centripetal rather than centrifugal -- it pulled inward on itself like a besieged army rather than spreading outward and diffusing its truth like leaven in a loaf. Thus, the primary literary genre for the fathers were apologies and attacks upon heretics. As part of this centering tendency, the writings of Justin and Irenaeus, forged on an anvil of conflict, became accepted as statements of the true faith.

The Latin-speaking churches of the west, no less than the Greek-speaking churches of the east, perceived themselves as continuously in combat with adversaries. The greatest of these early Latin soldiers of the faith was Tertullian (160 A.D. - 230 A.D.), the Carthagenian. The Latin mind tended to borrow its philosophy from the east -- its own interests and innovations lay in other areas -- and Tertullian simply took over Justin's Platonized theology of God's transcendence, now considered orthodox. He also follows Irenaeus in arguing that God's majesty demands that God be the sole uncreated and, therefore, creation comes out of nothing for there is nothing eternal but God alone. There is, however, a subtle difference in what Tertullian means by this now-hallowed formula. Tertullian, the Roman, was more of a Stoic than a Platonist; he believed the ultimate constitution of reality was matter, not spirit. Or, more precisely, when discussing the nature of God or the soul, he implies that spirit is really a very fine substance.

When coming upon the issue of the logos which bothered his Greek predecessors so much, Tertullian draws more on the Stoic image of pneuma than the middle-Platonic world-soul. For Tertullian, even more than for Justin and Irenaeus, the logos is inseparable from the world. God as pneuma already pervades everything as a finely-spun web for "all things are full of their author and occupied by him." As a divinely diffused substance, the logos is clearly a part of creation and so Tertullian accentuates an idea that Justin and Irenaeus asserted only reluctantly -- that the logos is created. Tertullian freely speaks of the logos as a creature. He solves the problem of the logos' divinity, not by reference to the middle-Platonic category of generation, but by the Stoic idea of substance. The logos is created but divine, for it cast from the stuff of divinity.

Thus, the Platonic distinction of two orders of reality became, for Tertullian, a Stoic distinction between two kinds of substances which renders meaningless the middle-Platonic image of a God beyond all finite categories. Substance is substance -- whether created or divine. Against Plato's sharp demarcation, Stoicism tended to see gradations of matter from the coarseness of the physical world to refinements of pneuma. The language of substance implies that God is not over and against the material world but is the highest state in a series of gradients. Tertullian's Stoicised cosmology is the flip-side of Plotinus'. Whereas Plotinus sees the spirit shading off into matter, or matter as a particularly unrefined form of spirit, Tertullian sees matter shading off into spirit or spirit as a particularly refined form of matter. As Plotinus broke with the dualism of Plato, whom he claimed to be copying, so Tertullian broke with the dualism of Justin, whom he claimed to be following.

Origen

If the Graeco-Roman world was an intellectual melting-pot, there is no place where it boiled more furiously than Alexandria. If one is to judge from his writings and those who comment on them, Origen (185 A.D. - 254 A.D.) grew up in a milieu fermenting with conflict among Jewish, Christian, Gnostic, Platonic, Stoic, and various idiosyncratic teachers like the elusive Ammonius Saccnas of whom Eusebius reports the (probably mistaken) rumor that both Origen and Plotinus were his pupils. In this highly volatile intellectual atmosphere where the most divisive and aggressive religious and philosophical schools debated and competed for adherents, Origen, and with him Christian theology, came to maturity.

Origen inherited the bastardized intellectual offspring of his forefathers. Unlike his predecessors, his primary impulse is not defensive but constructive. He wrote not so much to refute, oppose, or defeat but to create; especially, to create a coherent, Christian view of the world. Despite his intense philosophical mind, his focus was not speculative, but pastoral. His primary concern was salvation; the pilgrimage of the soul returning to its eternal source. Like Plato, Origen felt the central vocation of the soul is knowledge - not abstract cerebration, but contemplation which, for Origen, is the means of transformation and restoration.

If the soul's goal is return, it must have once departed. A problem which Justin and Irenaeus overlooked, and Origen saw clearly, concerned the soul's creation. If souls were created, as both Justin and Irenaeus insisted against the Platonic mainstream, how could they possess any affinity for the uncreated God? Origen takes over his predecessors' image of eternal generation and applies it to the soul as well as the logos; souls, too, are eternal, for their generation is without beginning. Having explained their closeness to God, Origen immediately faced another problem: If souls are eternal, how could they fall? Plato had blamed the fall on the distractions of matter but that made the body evil and the scripture said that creation was good. Justin argued that the souls fell from grace because they were created but that left inexplicable their rapport with the divine. How could the souls be eternal, yet mutable enough to sin?

Origen's solution was striking in its ingenuity. All souls were created equal, Origen taught; they inhabited a harmonious sphere in union with God. They are created, but eternally so; and being created, they are mutable, subject to change, transitory. Given their propensity to change, they revolted against God and fell from their orderly existence -- Origen takes the story of Adam and Eve as an allegory of the celestial fall of the eternal spirits. Not all souls, however, rejected God entirely; some only partially strayed and they fell (to use the metaphor spatially) only part way. From this comes the multiplicity of the cosmos. From the diversity of sin comes a diversity of bodies; Origen repeats the Platonic teaching on the variety of bodies a soul can inhabit -- celestial, astral, etheric, spiritual, and physical. The sun, moon, stars, and other celestial bodies are also souls, but souls who fell "less" than those found in physical bodies. The soul, on its fall, descends through these celestial, astral, and etheric realms to the earth and returns back through them on its upward journey home.

Matter arises at the fall as an expression of the diversity of souls. A brilliant move -- reversing Plato -- Origen has made sin the cause of matter rather than matter the cause of sin. Cosmology is wedded to soteriology: the physical universe is created and history ordained for the souls' transformation, to provide the experiences necessary for a return through growth in wisdom. The cosmos is constituted by this two-fold spiritual movement: downward from God into increasing materiality and upward toward God in contemplative transformation back into the likeness of its source. Being and becoming are not two incompatible worlds but two trajectories of cosmic motion, two paths on the soul's pilgrimage.

Beyond all speech, categories, theories, models, and images, Origen's God is essentialy unknowable. Beyond even "being", God "does not partake even in substance (ousia)" and transcends "all time, all ages, all eternity." While we cannot know God as he is in himself, we can know God as he manifests himself to us. The cosmos shows forth God's essential nature as creative and redemptive: cosmology is married to revelation. The universe is the light of God and, as with light, we see the rays but not the source, "The works of divine providence and the plan of the whole world are a sort of rays, as it were, of the nature of God." God is the fountainhead of being who "bestows upon all, existence" for all that is "has derived its being from Him." Love is self-giving and God is love, which means, for Origen, that he is eternally giving himself, eternally diffusing himself outward as the created order. This doctrine, later labeled "eternal creation," refers more to the nature of God than to the nature of the cosmos: God is eternal creativity, an endlessly overflowing expression of love and being; he is the timeless, spaceless singularity, the beginning point of a descending, diversifying and progressively returning river of existence. This transcendental creative energy is the source of that bi-polar movement which constitutes the universe: an emanation out from the source, and a reunion with it.

God's transcendence is <u>epistemic</u> but not <u>ontological</u>. God transcends human knowledge but not the great hierarchy of being. In the hierarchy of emanation, first comes God, the fountainhead eternal and uncreated. Out from him proceeds the logos-son, the everlasting form of all that comes after him. From the Father and the Son proceed the individual souls who form the cosmic community of rational spirits. From their fall, the physical cosmos arises. The logos is the divine creative will but, as Origen's predecessors found, the logos was intimately bound to creation. If the logos is eternally generated, so must be the rest of the cosmos. God's eternal creative will demands, according to Origen's logic, that God be eternally willing the creation. He writes in **First Principles**.

> So even God cannot be called omnipotent unless there exists something over whom he may exercise his power ....Therefore, that God might be shown to be almighty, it is necessary that all things should exist....but if there was never a time when he was not omnipotent, of necessity those things by which he receives the title must also exist and he must always have had those over whom he exercised power.

Origen insists that he agrees with Irenaeus that the world "was made and took its beginning in time" but this refers to this present world which is just one of many worlds of which there have been many before, and are many yet to come-- perhaps an eternal sequence of emanations and restorations.

Creation proceeds through the logos, the first-begotten of the cosmos. Jesus is the pattern according to which the rest of creation extrudes outward. He reveals, then, the true nature and destiny of the cosmos: It is a spiritual organism, diseased, but destined for what Origen calls "apocatastasis" -- the return of all things to their primal wholeness. This Origen said is what St. Paul meant by writing "God has made known to him his secret plan, which his will and pleasure decided on before hand, to be put into effect in the fullness of time, that the universe, all things in heaven and on earth, will be united together with Christ as the head." Jesus not only reveals this cosmic prospect; his death and resurrection assure its fulfillment. He has conquered the devil who stands, metaphorically, for all the powers which keep the soul from its return. "It was obvious to the eye," Origen wrote, "that the Son of God was crucified; what was not obvious to the eye was that the devil, too, was nailed to the cross with his principalities and power...the cross was the token born by Christ's victory over the devil." The death and resurrection of the logos-son is both the archetype and the cause of the apocatastasis of the cosmos; life coming out of death, victory coming after defeat, reunion following diversification until, as St Paul says, "God is all in all."

Soteriology, for Origen is broadened to include cosmology; matter plays an essential role in the drama of redemption. The physical cosmos is a direct manifestation of God's plan of restoration, and the providential structure of the universe provides the milieu through which the soul learns to journey home. Not the salvation of individuals alone, but the fall and restoration of the entire cosmos is the object of Origen's theodicy. Matter represents one stage in the spiritual history of the universe; it is the locus wherein the transcendent realm of spirit is externally expressed and diversified on its way back to harmony. The essential movement of the cosmos in all levels and facets is a going out and a coming back -- projection and introjection, individuation and reintegration -- an eternal oscillation of expression and recentering.

The Coming of the Trinity

In the classical world, physics and theology are inseparable. From Plato, through the Stoics and Albinus, to Plotinus and Origen, giving an account of the soul's redemption and the good life also involves providing an account of the physical world. Origen, however, was the last of the fathers who felt that cosmology was integral to a coherent explication of salvation. Even Augustine, (354-430 A.D.) whose <u>City of God</u> crowns the age of the fathers, and begins theology's middle ages, skips quickly over theories of cosmology (with a passing refutation of Origen's ideas) in order to focus on mankind as the primary object of redemptive history.

Augustine brought together two formerly separate philosophical traditions: Neo-Platonic mysticism with its emphasis upon contemplation of the transcendental ONE and Manicheanism, a dualistic school to which Augustine had briefly belonged as a youth, which emphasized the utter incompatibility of spirit and matter and the devaluation of the physical. Both impulses could look to Plato as their forefather and Augustine rejoined these divergent strands of post-platonic development - the monism of Plotinus and the dualism of the gnostics and Manicheans. While contemplation remained the goal of the soul, in Augustine's writings matter is regarded with the utmost suspicion and so it plays only a negative role in the economy of salvation. The popularity of Augustine, and his contemporary, the psuedonymous author books attributed to one Dionysius the Aeropagite, both of whom were heavily indebted to Plotinus, indelibly stamped a Plotinian mark upon medieval Christian mysticism. After Augustine, Christian mysticism would have both Neo-Platonic and dualistic overtones: the soul could be transformed and reunited to its source but the physical world must be left behind or even be apocalyptically destroyed rather than be transformed.

The increasing intellectual and political hegemony of the church after the emperor Constantine made Christianity the official religion of the empire in 313 AD freed it from any need to make its faith intelligible in terms of pagan science and enabled it to devote its intellectual energy exclusively to its own doctrinal preoccupations -- especially evolving a doctrine of God as Trinity, and Jesus as divine and human. The ultimate origin, however, of the Trinitarian controversies, lay in the cosmologies of Justin, Irenaeus, Tertullian, and Origen. All followed the Gospel of John in using the common cosmological term, logos, to explain the function of Christ, thereby importing into theology its various philosophical connotations over which they had no control. In both Stoicism and middle-Platonism, the logos or world-soul stood for the creative presence of the divine within the physical world. Thus, the continuing disputes over whether the logos-son was equal or subordinate to the father-God were also disputes over the relation of God and the world: Justin's mediating world-soul, Irenaeus' omnipresent divinity, Tertullian's gradations of substance, Origen's eternally generating logos, all express subtly different models of the relationship of creator and creature. After centuries of controversy over how the logos could be both created and fully divine, it fell to three fourth century theologians from Cappadocia (Gregory of Nyssa and his brother Basil and Gregory of Nazianzus) to define the formula declared orthodox forever and so put an end to the battle. Rather than think of the problem in terms of generation and origin (the created versus the uncreated) they conceptualized it in terms of essence. There are two essences -- divine and created. The difference between God and the world is not that one is uncreated and eternal and the other created and transitory, although that is certainly true, but that they have a different nature or essence (<u>ousia</u>). Thus, the traditional formula: a single divine essence existing in three hypostases -- Father, Son, Holy Spirit. Translated into Latin, it became three persons in one divine substance, an echo of Tertullian's Stoicism winning out in the end.

The Cappadocian interpretation of the creed associated with the Council of Nicaea (held in 325 A.D.) pictures a divine nature separate from and existing outside of the created world of time and space. God's transcendent nature is visualized in spatial and ontological terms -- a unique divine essence enthroned beyond the boundaries of the universe. Rather than the imagery of Origen and Plotinus, which capped generations of pagan and Christian development by perceiving reality as an integrated system of spirit flowing outward into matter and then reaching back to its source, one has the basis for a rather rigid and static two story model of a God separated from the world. The physical world was left theologically on its own, free to go its own way, irrelevant to the drama of redemption -- a drama increasingly centered on man alone. Origen's doctrine of apocatastasis was specifically condemned by Gregory of Nyssa, and later at the fifth general council of the church.

The immanence of God expressed in the imagery of the logos--the worldsoul, the cosmic mind, the indwelling spirit in the heart of the matter -- was central to the theology of the fathers. Justin needed it to mediate the transcedent God to the created order; Irenaeus needed it to refute the gnostic heresy of the irreconcilability of God and the world; Tertullian's Stoicism demanded the continuity of pneuma and creation; Origen's diffusive divinity envisioned the reciprocity of spirit and matter. Against Plato's rigid dualism, the basis of the gnostics condemnation of matter as evil, the fathers found in middle Platonism a powerful affirmation of the scriptural claim that creation was good. Matter is good, for it is the direct manifestation of an immanent divinity. The physical cosmos is a living reality, indwelt by a generative spirit. Matter is spirit projected outward; or, conversely, spirit is matter at its source. Not dead, the universe is pulsating with divine energy, driving it into existence, and propelling it towards redemption. The physical world is a soul on its way to reunion with its maker. Cosmology is an integral part of the history of salvation, for the entire universe is being transformed. All of this was swept away in the Cappadocian trinity, in which the logos-Son is removed from within the world, and firmly ensconced in the Godhead above. It falls to the Holy Spirit -- the neglected member of the triune deity -- to carry the functions of divine immanence. Gregory of Nyssa decribed the spirit as the presence of God within creation in ways almost reminiscent of Irenaeus and Origen. But such immanence remains theoretically problematic and incoherent; Gregory could never explain how the created and uncreated essences interact. Precisely this problem led his descendents into generations of warfare over the person of Christ. The driving force of the Cappadocian solution was transcendence, not immanence -- a divine essence over-against all finite substance. A dualism, Platonic in its rigidity, returned to haunt Christian theology. The heritage of the Nicene Creed is a potentate God, who ruled his creation from afar rather than an indwelling spirit of love, forever giving itself in the heart of the cosmos, more a God of power than of presence.

Middle-Platonism solved the problem of what would, in more scholastic times, be called God's immanence and transcendence in a typically plural way

-- two Gods. Justin felt his monotheism would not allow him to say this, but he tried anyway. For the next three centuries, evolving the doctrine of the Trinity was, on one level, the struggle to say what Justin found impossible, and to bind together many contradictory assertions -- that there is a transcendent God (Father) and an immanent logos (Son); they are both the same God, but not exactly the same, since one is uncreated and the other created, yet somehow the created one is still divine. The Cappadocian resolution simplified the matter by rejecting the early fathers' image of eternal generation, and directly calling the Son and Spirit too uncreated. In setting the three persons made of one uncreated substance apart from the finite world, Justin's impulse towards transcendence and the uncompromising monotheism of the Old Testament are preserved, lost is the fathers' reciprocal relation between spirit and matter. The simplicity of the image of the tri-part deity came by sacrificing the divine immanence within matter. Bereft of the <u>logos spermatikos</u> (the seeds of divinity sown by Stoicism and middle-Platonism), the physical world is purely finite, material and transitory; divinity is to be sought beyond the sky. Thus, the theological understanding of matter and nature -- a task to which the greatest minds of the pagan and early patristic eras set themselves -- becomes increasingly problematic and unnecessary. The loss of a spiritual and theological vision of nature was the price paid for the doctrine of the Trinity.

CHAPTER THREE:

TOWARD A MATERIAL SPIRITUALITY

Classical Alchemy: Philosophical Background

The impulse towards a spiritual understanding of matter did not die with the coming of the Trinity; it persisted, slightly underground, in the alchemical community. A complex tradition of ancient lineage, alchemy is really several variations on a common theme. In the classical period, there was no peculiarly alchemical philosophy. The outlook of the alchemist was common to all. To most ancient scientists, the world was composed of a single universal substance existing in several forms: For Thales, the primal "stuff" was water; for Anaximander, it was qualityless essence; for Anximenes, and later the Stoics, it was <u>pneuma</u>; for Aristotle, it was the <u>prima materia.</u> This was the principle of unity; multiplicity arose from the permutations of four basic elements; for Thales they were wetness, dryness, heat, cold; for Empedokles they were solid, liquid, gaseous, and fiery. Plato, with his penchant for geometry, called the four governing forms triangular, cubical, octahedronal, and icosahedronal, which he correlated with Empedokles' fire, solid, gas, and liquid. Aristotle superimposed the two sets of four which he inherited, and got four combinations: hot and dry, hot and wet, cold and wet, and cold and dry -- which he equated with the four primal elements of fire, air, water, and earth.

While his predecessors saw the basal element in static terms, Plato, by consciously conceiving of matter by analogy with geometric forms, argued for a radically different image -- <u>transformation</u>. Triangles can be joined into pryamids, which can then be transposed into eight-sided octahedrons, which can then be expanded by additional triangles into a twenty-faced icosahedron. Likewise, Plato reasoned, the primal elements can be reorganized and recombined, thus transmuting matter. Aristotle, with his eye on the way species grow and decay, picked up Plato's idea of transformation. Building on Empedokles, and conceiving of the world as a combination of four interacting polarities -- earth, air, fire, and water, Aristotle envisioned the transmutation of substances taking place by an alteration in the polar patterns of interaction. Matter exhibits both continuity and change: A universal, unchanging substance forms itself into a kaleidoscope of shapes, according to definite patterns.

Beginning with organisms rather than geometry, Aristotle introduced another image -- one that would have seemed unnecessary to Plato -- teleology. Change takes place not only in repetition of invariant forms but also in motion towards a goal. A pile of bricks may be transformed into a house, according to the mathematical formula of the architect's plan, but plans are governed by a higher principle of function. Bricks are put together in an orderly way, not only to satisfy aesthetic tastes, but also, so that the mass of mortar can function as a house. Seeds and embryos develop towards a goal and minerals are to be understood by analogy with living organisms, rather than understanding living organisms by analogy with minerals. Minerals and ores and chemical elements, too, grow towards an end. Aristotle did not see the cosmos as a whole developing but he conceived of ores and elements developmentally. Thus, the ancients thought that metals grew in the bowels of the earth as roots spread out from a seed and that if ore was mined out, in time it would grow back like a pruned branch.

Gold is the metallic summum bonum: luxurious and maleable, it is a gift from the gods, a sign of power, the essence of wealth and status. The compulsion to possess gold was common in the ancient world; the dream of finding it, or better yet, producing it, was well-nigh universal. In Homer's Odyssey is a passage hinting that the goddess Athena transforms silver to gold. Pliny, the Roman historian, recounts how a preceptor named Gaius attempted to produce gold by chemical concoction, but "he suffered loss". Increasingly throughout the Roman period, tales circulated, often originating in Egypt, about various mechanical and magical attempts at making gold from some cheaper substance.

Seeing the cosmos as an interlocking system resulted in numerous theories correlating events from various parts of the whole. The most complex and popular of these was astrology. If stars and men are parts of the same scheme then there must be some connection between celestial and earthly happenings. The search for such connections and regularities made astrology one of the chief sciences of the ancient world. One correlation made early was between metals and heavenly bodies. Each metal became linked to a star or planet; men dreamed of finding the secret of metal among the stars and the celestial hierarchy became assimilated to a metallic one. Celsus, in his second century attack on Christianity, repeats a common belief in the soul's descent and ascent along a spiritual ladder of seven rungs, made in turn of lead, tin, copper, iron, an alloy, silver, and finally, gold, which he connects with various heavenly bodies culminating in the moon for silver, and the sun for gold. Origen, Celsus' adversary, uses the same image of the soul climbing down, and then up, this ladder. Iamblichus, a neo-Platonist writing at the turn of the fourth century, describes the purification of the soul with the imagery of smelting so that "all that is in us becomes like to gold, just as the fire assimilates all hard and solid objects to subtle and luminous bodies." By the second century, a period engulfed with concern about the soul's development, it was common to join together images for the transformation of the psyche, the transmutation of metals, and the rotation of the heavens.

Such imagery was already in use in Christian circles. The Bible speaks of the refiner's fire with a double intention: the image refers both to the smelting of metals, and to the fiery presence of God, which purifies the soul. The New Testament mentions a baptism by fire, and the Greek word "baptism" has its origin in the ancient, pre-alchemical crafts of smelting and dyeing, referring to transforming material by submerging it in dye or other chemicals. When the revered and aged Polycarp, the last survivor of the generation who had known the apostles, was burned at the stake, his martyrdom was described as "gold and silver being purified in the furnace". A fifth century Christian treatise on the resurrection of the body draws directly on the imagery of alchemy. Whereas St. Paul had said that the resurrected body was to the earthly body as a tree to its seed, the author of this treatise (Aineas of Gaza) says the resurrection is "as if an artisan gathers the fragments [of metal], purifies them, and by a singular science, transforms them into gold....Thus behaves the matter of the perishable and corruptible body, which by the creative art becomes pure and beautiful."

Even more striking is the illustration used by the renowned eighth century preacher, John of

Damascus. Describing how the finite and physical human being can draw near to God, he says,

> It is just the same as when lead and gold are exiled far apart, a distance yawns between their homes, a vastness separates them. A certain craftsman then might come and seek to show his skill, the operation of his art, his scientific lore; he'd take the lead and melt it down inside his fiery furnace, he'd show the lead transformed to gold, the best in quality.

In the first centuries of the church's development, then, it was common to understand death, beginning with martyrdom, as an alchemical transformation. Neo-Platonists, who thought only in terms of the journey of the soul, applied this imagery to its transformation so that its return to the Source was like lead being purified into "subtle and luminous" gold. Christianity, with its doctrine of the resurrection of the body, saw the resurrection as a transmutation. St. Paul said the physical body becomes a spiritual body as a seed becomes a plant; the fathers said it was more like lead being made into gold.

Almost universally, then, Ionian natural philosophy contained three elements: an essence from which all is made, a theory of four primal elements arranged as poles in opposition, a structure by which the variety of matter is constituted by the combination of primal atoms, geometrical forms, or opposing forces. There was little differentiation between mineral and vegetable realms: Ores were born, developed, and replenished themselves like plants. Alongside this was the natural thirst for precious metals and for knowledge about the fate of the soul. The soul was envisioned in a cosmic, astrological context in which its transformation was likened to physical and astronomical processes. All of this implied that the transmutation of one metal to another was theoretically possible; all that was lacking was the correct technique.

Classical Alchemy: Technical Background

The alchemical impulse was mother to the invention of much of the apparatus used by chemists to this day. From the vast blast-furnaces that smelt tons of metal in a single gulp to the most delicate glass retorts and condensers, most are offspring of the alchemists' ingenuity. The transmutation of stone into molten and hardened forms goes back at least to 4000 B.C.. The process we call smelting was first applied to copper and bronze, and only much later (around 1200 B.C.) to iron. From the first, the application of fire to ore took place in a ritualized atmosphere; ancient metallurgy was an alloy of technique, ritual, and magic comprehended by myth. Those who knew the secret of producing metal from stone were on a par with those who knew the mystery of the soul or how to govern men; secrecy and initiation existed in the metal workers' guild (as in the temple priesthood and ruling caste). From the earliest days of civilization, men have known that fire is an agent of transformation and its control through the perfection of the furnace was a major techno-spiritual advance. The Babylonians, Assyrians, and Akadians continually produced recipes for making alloys, glass, and smelting and fusing metals. All the ancient civilizations had sophisticated techniques for refining gold and silver and separating metals. The Egyptians, who had the most abundant supply of gold in the ancient world, perfected the metallurgical techniques to use it in inlays, jewelry, and utensils.

Demockritos, the fifth century B. C. Greek guru known as one of the fathers of atomism, was fascinated by the interaction of color, temperature, and metallic quality. While Demockritos' character is well-fortified with legend, he appears to have been interested in the transmutation of metals and understood atomic theory as a means to explain it. Substances being a combination of atoms, if the combination changes, the substance does, too. He may also have performed some experiments to demonstrate in light of his theory what had been known for centuries -- through the application of heat, dye, or chemical, substances could be transformed or at least change their appearance.

Bollos of Mendes (second century B. C.) stood in the same tradition; he may even have ascribed his writings to Demockritos. The sayings attributed to him mix magical lore with textbook formulas for transmuting metals and making gold. He wrote essays on dyeing and alloying: The application of heat or dye were the major tools of Bollos' craft. Bollos sought a solvent through which all elements could be dissolved and reduced to their essence. Thus, he hoped to find the "single nature that suffices to conquer All", the primal matter, the essence of essences. For Bollos, the knowledge needed to transmute metal was common in antiquity, but lost in the present. He had gone to Egypt to learn the lore of the ancients, but no one knew it. He describes finding the lost books of wisdon hidden in a temple pillar when the column miraculously cracked open before him. Finding the secret was as much a part of the alchemical trade as perfecting the apparatus.

It was natural for Bollos to go to Egypt for there the long tradition of metallurgy, the intense philosophical climate, and the insatiable soteriological drive first fused into alchemy. There the conjunction of speculative cosmology and practical metal-working reached its summit in the work of one of Egypt's daughters -- Maria the prophet, a Jewish woman of Alexandria, and by legend, Miriam, the sister of Moses, although she lived in the first century A.D.. Classical alchemy never surpassed her inventive genius and speculative power. She fashioned the equipment by which chemistry conducted itself for over two thousand years. Her most brilliant appliance was a three-armed still which she made from copper, having invented a technique for making tubes from sheet metal. She also devised two of the most popular furnaces, which were still in use at the beginning of modern science. It is well into the eighteenth century before any retorts or condensers surpass her design. Her aphorisms which have survived dwell on a "divine water" which is the soul; also an angel, the vital principle of creation. Rain falls, evaporates, distills, condenses -- providing Maria with an apt image for the transmutation of metal through many stages. By continually heating and cooling, she tried to distill the essence of matter.

By the fourth century A. D., alchemy has acquired a substantial body of theoretical lore and textbook formulae. It falls to one Zosimos to synthesize this heritage. Called by later alchemists the "crown of philosophy", neither theoretically nor technically does his work surpass that of Maria but his twenty eight volume encyclopedia is a monmument of alchemical teaching. He records experiments, formulae, instructions on building furnaces and appliances, and speculations on the primal secret known to the ancients and passed down by a sealed fraternity. He zdraws liberally from the writings of Jews and Christians while remaining convinced that alchemy is the primitive tradition from which all religions spring. The soul is saved not by ritual practice nor ascetic denial, but by disciplined involvement in the processes of nature. The cosmic spirit spoken about in Neo-Platonism manifests itself through nature and alchemy allows one to participate in this spiritual motion: By learning how to transmute metal, one transforms the soul.

From the ancient experimenters like Demockritos and Bollos through the artisans of the laboratory like Maria and Zosimos, the methods perfected over millennia in the guilds become fused with cosmological and soteriological interests. Yet, these alchemists never forget their roots; they remain basically men and women of the fire and the bench. It is practical wisdom that they seek. The soteriological struggle to free the soul from illusion and necessity is captive to the concrete struggle to transmute lesser metals into gold. Classical philosophy intimated that such change is theoretically possible; these heirs of the ancient guilds sought to demonstrate that it is practically possible as well. Sharing the longing of their age for a recipe for salvation, the only recipe they thought worthy of the name is one worked out in the furnaces and the retort.

The Great Work

The alchemical tree has many roots: Ancient theories of metals as living organisms and elements as permutations of a primal substance, techniques refined over generations in craft fraternities, the quest for spiritual truth in an ethos where matter and spirit are joined, the lust for gold and precious metals. The tree was also pruned: In 292 A. D., the Roman emperor Diocletion expelled the alchemists from Egypt and burned their books; Christian emperors and bishops looked on alchemy with a suspicious and persecutorial eye, and the Christian emperors Constantine and Valintinian I repeated the edict of Diocletion; the Moslems swept through Alexandria and burned its library. Thus was lost to western sight the vision of Plato, the investigations of Aristotle, the ecstasy of Plotinus, the apparatus of Maria. Borne by invading and returning Islamic armies, the knowledge spread east, and the tree took root there and grew. For centuries, the Arabic philosophers and experimenters, culminating in Jabir (eighth century) perfected the Hermetic wisdom and technology. During the twelfth century, the Moslem conquerors were driven out of Europe; their universities and manuscripts were left behind, translated, and studied. Through this three-fold process of translation -- from Greek to Arabic to Latin -- Europeans again learned of Plato, Aristotle, and alchemy.

On February 11, 1144, Robert of Chester, Abbot of a Spanish monastery, an avid investigator into mathematics and astronomy, published his translation of Arabic alchemical material, The Book of the Composition of Alchemy. Almost a century of alchemical translation followed, as well as the reappropriation of the Greek writings of Plato and Aristotle. In the thirteenth century, a stage full of figures -- like Roger Bacon, Arnold of Villanova, Albertus Magnus -- all devout churchmen, all insatiably and scientifically curious, all engrossed in alchemy -- entered the scene. Bacon, a Franciscan friar whoses experimental methodology set the course for modern science, attempted to use the experimental approach to perfect the alchemical search. Arnold, also caught up in laboratory research, saw alchemy as a material mysticism, whereby stages of transfromation which metals undergo on their way to becoming gold parallel the stages of Christ's earthly life, and of the soul's pilgrimage towards illumination. Albertus Magnus, probably the most respected theologian of his era, wrote widely on alchemy and performed fundamental experiments on several crucial chemical substances, in addition to his extensive theological authorship. His pupil, Thomas Aquinas, whose Summa Theologica dominated late medieval scholasticism and remains authoritative for Roman Catholics to this day, was convinced that the structure of matter could be alchemically transformed. Thus, alchemy is firmly entrenched in the theological and scientific sensibilities of the middle ages.

Alchemy is governed by the vision of transformation: Of lesser into higher metals, of matter into spirit, of the soul into greater purity. This overarching schema is expressed in several concrete images -- the philosopher's stone, the Magnum Opus, the elixer of life, and a host of minor ones -- all of which intermingle material and spiritual concerns. More than a method, alchemy is a pilgrimage. One travels to learn the secret -- Nicholas Flamel traversed Spain, seeking someone who could decode the manuscript he had found; John Dee crossed the ocean between England and the continent several times; Paracelsus was a peripatetic student and teacher. Then one works incessantly to master the techniques: In the process the soul, gaining wisdom and maturity, approaches the ultimate destination of enlightenment and immortality. The <u>Magnum Opus</u> is both the journey and its goal: Any work of spiritual development is a <u>Magnum Opus</u>, involving suffering, pain, labor, death, and finally, rebirth. The alchemist undergoes the same process of transformation as his chemicals. Alchemy is not an objective science with an experimenter detached from his experiment, but is rather a single process of transformation in which both the chemist and the chemicals are involved together.

To the medieval alchemist, this process is essentially spiritual. The laboratory and the chapel stand side by side; no experiment is undertaken without prayer and fasting. Before he can purify metals, the alchemist must pruify himself. The famous (and, according to rumor, successful) fourteenth century alchemist, Nicholas Flamel, wrote this prayer with which to begin his work:

> All-powerful God, father of light, from whom come all good and perfect gifts, I beg thy infinite mercy; grant that I may know thy eternal wisdom, that wisdom that surrounds thy throne, which creatd and perfected, guides and keeps all things. I pray that thou mayest send it unto me from heaven, thy sanctuary, and from the throne of thy glory, that it may be and work in me. For it is thy wisdom that governs all celestial and occult arts, that keeps the knowledge and intelligence of all things. Grant that it may accompany me in all my works; that by its spirit I may have true knowledge; that I may proceed without error in the noble art to which I have dedicated myself.

Another alchemist writes, "False alchemists seek only to make gold; true philosophers desire only knowledge." Elias Ashmole, the seventeenth century English alchemist, describes the "adept" as one who...

> being a lover of wisdom more than worldy wealth, drove at higher and more excellent operations:

and certainly he to whom the whole course of nature lies open, rejoiceth not so much that he can make gold and silver, or the devils to become subject to him, as that he sees the heavens open, the angels of God ascending and descending, and that his own name is fairly written in the book of life.

The alchemical drive is spiritual and soteriological. The wisdom sought is not a chemical recipe, but rather "the principle of all things". The goal is comprehending the most primal structures of the universe, and since these are assuredly spiritual, the alchemist knows:

> Our art, its theory as well as its practice, is altogether a gift of God, who gives it when and to whom He elects: It is not of him that wills or of him that runs, but simply through the mercy of God.

The alchemist seeks to understand matter fundamentally, and that, for him, means spiritually; alchemical knowledge is more revelation than invention.

The alchemist also feels that the proof of the pudding is in the eating, not the cooking. The spirituality sought is practical. Understanding is not enough: neither the contemplation of divine beauty nor the ecstasy of transcendental intuition. Wisdom must be proven in the heat of the furnace and the bubbling retorts. Laboratory experiment and spiritual experience are two sides of the same process; alchemy compliments the traditionally spiritual view of matter by experimental and technological methods. Authentic spiritual wisdom comes not from ascetic withdrawl, but by daily intercourse with the physical world. Spirituality arises from matter, and acts back upon it by transforming it; true spirituality is gained and tested in the laboratory.

Whenever spirituality is understood as a process of transformation, it is called upon to show that something is transformed. In the eighteenth and nineteenth centuries, spiritual experience proved itself by the transformation of moral character, just as today it is called upon to aid in the transformation of the personal psyche. In the Victorian era, a good moral character was worth more than gold (or so people said) and so, true spirituality was that which transmuted a degenerate sinner into a virtuous citizen. Today, a healthy psyche is the highest good, and so authentic spirituality must guarantee a well-integrated personality. (Thus, it is no accident that the most brilliant exponent of this value in the modern age, C. Jung, has written extensively on Hermetic texts and sees psychiatry and spirituality as kindred forms of alchemy.) Since spirit and matter are linked in the classical world, the transformation most ardently sought by the medieval age was that of the physical creation and alchemy sought to prove its spiritual power by the transmutation of metal.

The physics with which the medieval alchemist worked was that of Aristotle, for alchemy re-entered Europe with the rediscovery of Aristotle, both from Arabic sources. <u>Prima Materia</u> was driven into multiplicity by the mutual interaction of four elements (earth, air, fire, water) and four qualities (hot, cold, wet, dry). If their pattern of interaction and proportion changes, substance mutates. Aristotle also theorized that ores were living substances which grew primarily by the impact of the heavenly bodies, as the sun's rays make leaves and flowers come out. Astrology expresses this link between the rest of the cosmos and the earth; everything that happens on earth is paralleled celestially. A correct understanding of the seasons and stars is as important as the correct theory of chemical composition. Just as the farmer must know to plant in the spring and harvest in the fall, the alchemist must sow his chemical seeds when the moon and stars are in the correct season. Theologically, alchemy was indebeted to Neo-Platonism. This complex series of interactions -- metal to metal, star to chemical, experimenters to experiment -- is pervaded and governed by an orderly and harmonious divine Spirit. This Spirit holds the secret of the universe, and it is this Spirit and the correspondence which it generates which the alchemist sees incarnate in the philosophers' stone.

The mutual interaction of spirit and matter guides the alchemical journey. The basic alchemical maxim is that "bodies must become incorporal" -- that is, matter must be distilled back into spirit. But, unlike Platonism, the trajectory of alchemy is not away from matter, but more deeply into it. Sir George Ripley, a fifteenth century Canon of the English church and respected figure in his own day, sums up the core of the alchemical process in three statements.

> The first is that the body must be made Spiritual. The second is that the Spirit must be made corporal and fused with it and become consubstantial. The third reason is that it may be purged from its original impurity.

This can be taken both as an allegorical account of a laboratory procedure (spirit and body standing for chemicals) and as a soteriological vision of apocatastasis when matter and spirit are transformed, purified, and conjoined.

The father's identification of Jesus with the logos, the cosmic governing principle, makes possible the equation of the philosophers' stone with Christ: both incarnate the fundamental structure of the universe. The alchemical process correlates with the soul's development, and the passion of Christ is an analogue for both. Chemicals are said to suffer and to die in the vessel aptly named the crucible -- one famous alchemical illustration has the element mercury in the form of a snake nailed to a cross. Likewise, in medieval spirituality, suffering is an important part of the purification of the soul. The central images of spiritual purification -- baptism and the refiners' fire -- both have roots in ancient alchemy. The final purification is death. Chemicals must undergo their Good Friday and Holy Saturday for "nothing can be reborn to a better state unless it has first died and gone through a period of dissolution and putrification of its previous principles." If the alchemist has done his work right, a crucial stage in the transmutation of metal occurs when the chemicals turn to black, symbolizing death: The soul, too, on its pilgrimage, enters what St. John of the Cross calls the black night where it dies to its selfish desires. Following death comes rebirth. Jesus arises from his tomb, and before the experimenter's astonished eyes, the charred mass of his experiment has its Easter and comes to life as pure gold. Having suffered its dark night, the soul, too, enters enlightenment. Whereas the early fathers describe the the resurrection with alchemical imagery, the medieval alchemists describe their science in the language of resurrection. Jesus -- the logos of the fathers -- has become the archetype of all transformations:

Souls and chemicals enter a common transfiguring sequence of suffering, death, and rebirth; the redemptive drama is played out in the beakers and stills; the cross and resurrection are imprinted on matter.

Origen taught that Christ redeemed the whole cosmos, but by the middle ages, the benefits of Christ's sacrifice were applied exclusively to human history. In alchemy, the impulse towards a physical soteriology continues. Jesus saved mankind, alchemy redeems nature. Alchemy is the extension of the incarnation into the physical world. The alchemist is a co-redeemer and co-worker with God. Since minerals develop organically into gold, the alchemist, by his spiritual technology, speeds up the cosmic processes. As Eliade says, the alchemist "takes up and perfects the work of nature." The <u>Magnum Opus</u> is a hastening of the apocatastasis.

Ancient physicists conceived of matter as a common essence diversifying itself according to set quadrilateral patterns. To later alchemists, this <u>prima materia</u> was the Neo-Platonic universal spirit. Not content with Plotinian contemplation, the alchemist applied cosmic wisdom to mundane elements. By understanding the laws of physical transformation, the adept becomes the locus of spiritual transformation. The spiritual energy which pervades and powers the zodiac in its revolutions, plants in their flowering, chemicals in their interactions, can be grasped and focused by human consciousness, like a lens focusing the sun, and directed at the redemption of the universe. Consciousness is the matrix of transformation. Through the search for alchemical wisdom -- years of pouring over antique manuscripts, decades of stoking the fire and minding the retort -- the adept expands, disciplines, and matures his consciousness until it is a fit crucible for the transformation of matter.

Alchemy in the Seventeenth Century

From the twelfth through the seventeenth century, there is an increasing torrent of alchemical publications, and no one could consider themselves educated in the sixteenth or seventeenth centuries who had not studied some basic alchmical texts. By then, however, the marriage of spirituality and technology, which made alchemy distinctive, was showing signs of divorce. Some, like the seventeenth century French Jesuit, Mersenne, attack alchemy as a virulent threat to orthodox religion and practical science. His English contemporary, Francis Bacon, carried on the same polemic against the secret and esoteric aspects of alchemy, while himself peforming many alchemical procedures, and fully believing in the transmutation of metals. In 1661, Robert Boyle published his Skeptical Chymist, climaxing the assault of Mersenne and Bacon. Boyle rejected the physics of Aristotle and the recipes of the alchemists, insisting instead on public and repeatable experiments. Boyle, however, remained convinced of the possibility of transmutation.

Secrecy had been endemic to alchemy since its birth in the ancient guilds for whom secret knowledge is power and who feared the adulteration of their skills through popularization. Medieval alchemy was closely tied with spiritual discipline and the individual's personal maturity was more important to completing the Magnum Opus than familiarity with ancient recipes. By the seventeenth century, men insisted that knowledge be public and impersonal, and thus was born the myth of objectivity which has dominated the modern age with its illusion that knowledge can ultimately be separated from the knower. The offspring of objectivity was technology, with its stress on the perfectability of the machine and the interchangeability of the worker. In the days of the guilds, if one sought to make a better chair (for example) one perfected one's personal skill. Today, if we want a better product, we perfect the machine which anyone can operate without any disciplined personal development. This drive towards the most public, common, and impersonal forms of knowledge killed alchemy, rather than the failure of its experiments or the development of atomic chemistry. The impulse towards the impersonal necessitated the failure of alchemical experiments. When they did not produce gold, the experimenters, imbued with the new notions of knowledge, blamed the experiment, and not their spiritual immaturity.

The secret and esoteric aspects of alchemy are not ends in themselves but symptoms of the fact that alchemy is personal knowledge par excellence. Alchemy attempted to keep the power to transform the world in tandem with the maturity of those who hold it. When men increasingly valued the comprehension and transformation of the universe without any corresponding need to comprehend and transform themselves, objectivity was born and alchemy died. In 1658, Boyle capped the arguments of Mersenne and Bacon against the secrecy of alchemy by writing an essay advocating that all knowledge be made public. Issac Newton, who by that time had claimed some successes in the alchemical laboratory, wrote the Secretary of the Royal Society that Boyle should remain silent. Apparently, Newton knew that alchemy contained "other things besides ye transmutation of metalls" which could not be revealed.

Throughout the seventeenth century, alchemy was subdividing: becoming either increasingly spiritual and decreasingly experimental, like the Rosicrucians and theosophy, in which a unified metaphysical cosmology developed with little accompanying struggle in the laboratory; or increasingly experimental and less spiritual where tracking experiments overwhelmed prayer and meditation. Belief in the transmutation of metal continued throughout the century, but this was never the essence of alchemy. Shorn of its spiritual connotations, alchemy was increasingly rephrased in the mechanistic and experimental languages of Descartes, Leibniz, Bacon, and Boyle. Gradually, the ancient recipes proved fruitless for the new experimental chemists, and were discarded, leaving a mystical consciousness to live on in isolation from the physical workd. In the carefully monitored experiments of Oxford and Cambridge and the lush and secret initiation rites of the Rosicrucians, the alchemical impulse towards synthesis was lost. Men awakened to the new dawn of the age of reason, forgetting the primal dream of integrating spirit and matter.

Not lost was the dream of understanding the world as the interaction of principles and forces. This task now fell primarily to Isaac Newton. Like most of his contemporaries, Newton felt that if alchemy was approached in a more orderly way, it would yield the answer to the riddle of the cosmos. He spent much of his time copying alchemical texts and laborously devising relevant laboratory procedures and in unpublished manuscripts claimed numerous alchemical achievements, including the production of "philosophical mercury." Beyond that, his most fundamental mechanical principles can be seen as transmutations of alchemical concepts: "aether" is a mechanization of the Neo-Platonic universal spirit, in which Newton devoutly believed: "force" a mechanizing of the sympathetic attraction between bodies so dear to astrology -- e.g., gravity comes from <u>gravitas</u>, a Latin word meaning heavy and a common alchemical term for lead and for the planet Saturn. To the end of his life, Newton struggled to integrate the ancient alchemical heritage with the new mechanical philosophy and his physics represents the translation of alchemy into mechanical terms. In the next century the offspring would kill its parent: the mechanical imagery, in which Newton cast alchemy in an attempt to save it, completely overwhelmed its hermetic inheritance. From the death of alchemy as a natural philosophy, an event Newton would have abhorred, "newtonian" science was born.

CHAPTER FOUR:

THE RETURN TO DUALISM

Mid-Wives to the Machine.

In the middle of the second century A.D., Ptolemy of Alexandria published what was to be the classical textbook of astronomy, arguing that the earth stood still and the heavenly bodies were attached to a crystalline sphere which rotated the earth once every twenty-four hours. Some stars appeared fixed in the course of this rotation; others appeared to move in a more erratic way, with an annual as well as daily pattern. These erratic movements of the bodies we call planets could be explained by putting the sun at rest and the earth in motion about it. Aristarchos of Somoas, in the third century B.C., had proposed this heliocentric view but classical science rejected it. Men knew the required motion would be so great that it would disrupt life on earth -- stones would not fall in straight lines and the air would be in constant turbulence. Also, if the earth moved, it should appear in displacement relative to the fixed stars -- as a house appears differently as we walk around it -- but no such motion could be found. So telling was this objection that, centuries later, the greatest stellar observer in human history, Tycho Brahe, wanted to accept the heliocentric view but could not because he could find no evidence of the earth's action relative to the fixed stars. So the heliocentric view was rejected and Ptolemy proposed instead that the planets move in two orbits: a major orbit around the earth on which a point can be located and then the planet itself revolves around this point in a smaller orbit called an epicycle. The planets move in a circular orbit which itself orbits the earth; thus, the planets can appear to go temporarily backward or suddenly forward.

By the middle ages, this Ptolemaic vision had been amalagmated with Aristotle's cosmology and Christian theology to form an integrated model of the cosmos. The earth is the center, reflecting both Ptolemy's calculations and a theology which saw the fall and restoration of mankind as the unique object of God's activity. The special nature of human existence -- for mankind is alone created "in the image of God" and the recipient of Christ's sacrifice -- is reflected cosmologically in mankind's home being the center of the universe. The Platonic-Aristotelian perfection of the circle entails that the universe is a series of spheres or circles: The sun, the moon, and the planets rotate the earth in perfect circularity, the fixed stars, constellations and zodiac are attached to a sphere which marks the outer boundaries of the universe. Literally beyond this sphere sits the transcendent Trinity on their sapphire thrones, surrounded by the souls blessed in paradise. Following Aristotle, Thomas Aquinas insisted that this cosmic organization represents a hierarchy of beings: Stars and planets are more "heavenly;" closer to God, they are made of "heavenly" material and obey "heavenly" laws. Immutable and eternal, they are distinct from the matter and organization of the imperfect and corruptible earth. Theology and cosmology reinforced each other in a grand design.

As more accurate observations are made, more elaborate modifications are necessary to make the Ptolemaic system work. By the beginning of the sixteenth century, Nicholos Copernicus (1473-1543), a minor ecclesiastical official and mathematician, had grown dissatisifed with the ever-complexifying schema of Ptolemy. Far from being an enemy of the faith, Copernicus held minor orders in the Catholic church and apparently felt that a wise God would not have made such a cumbersome cosmos. He had no desire to remove mankind from the center of God's providence nor to attack the wisdom of Aristotle and Plato. Rather, being a mathematician like Plato, he accepted the major premise of ancient wisdom -- the perfection of the circle. It was Ptolemy with his epicycles within epicycles who had deviated from the simplicity and elegance of the ancestors. Wanting to vindicate tradition, not destroy it, this canon of the church developed a system in which all the heavenly bodies moved in perfect circles -- but they went around the sun instead of the earth. Copernicus knew that the claim that earth moved flew in the face of common sense and was wild and irrational. Hence, he hesitated to publish his work. It was only on the urging of many, including a Papal emissary and cardinal of the church, that Canon Copernicus published The Revolution of Celestial Orbits in 1543. It was dedicated to the Pope, who surely knew of its contents in advance; no one in the church made any move to suppress his hypothesis that all the planets, including the earth, moved in a double motion -- in an orbit around the stationary sun and in rotation around their axis.

Copernicus was a mathematician by trade and his problems with Ptolemy were theoretical and not empirical. Lack of regularity and elegance troubled Copernicus more than agreement with observations. Because Copernicus insisted, like Ptolemy and Aristotle before him, that heavenly bodies must move in perfect circles, his system did not fit the observational accounts any better than his rivals. But it was simpler and more regular. Beyond that, Copernicus was harkening back to a tradition earlier than Aristotle -- to Plato and the Pythagoreans -- that geometry holds the key to cosmology. The universe is an orderly, interdependent, coherent system of relationships which are mathematically explicable. Nothing in nature says that nature must be coherent and follow the patterns of human, mathematical construction; but Copernicus, like Plato, was convinced that mathematics was the image of reality and perfection. Armed with this unswerving faith in God as a geometer, he defied common sense and empirical observation and preserved the geometric ideals of regularity and simplicity by putting the earth in motion around the sun.

Of precisely the opposite temperament was Tycho Brahe (1546-1601). Whereas Copernicus was shy and retiring, Brahe was boastful and contentious; whereas Copernicus was lured into the heavens by a vision of pure, mathematical simplicity, Brahe engaged in the tedious task of making thousands upon thousands of minute observations. Wedded to common sense, Brahe was unconvinced by Copernicus and set to make new observations which would defend the old system. His new and more accurate data fit neither system and so he devised one of his own in which he sought the best of both worlds: the planets revolved around the sun, and this whole system in turn rotated the earth; thus, he preserved the theologically essential feature of the traditional model -- the centrality of the earth -- while maintaining the scientifically essential feature of Copernicus' theory -- the movement of the planets around the sun. Empirically, it fit the data at least as well as the hypothesis of Copernicus, and was no threat to medieval sensibility. It was cumbersome in the extreme but that did not bother one whose impulses were not at all theoretical.

Johannes Kepler (1571-1630) was convinced by Copernicus but was Brahe's associate. Like Copernicus, he was first and foremost a mathematician and favored elegance over observation, and so was drawn by the simplicity of the Copernican and opposed to the complexities of the Ptolematic and Tychonic systems. At Brahe's death-bed, Kepler inherited the lifetime of observations made to support the geocentric system, and he used them to defend Copernicus. Kepler did it by sacrificing the ancient ideal of the circle; if the planets were envisioned in eliptical orbits, Brahe's observations fit Copernicus' system almost exactly.

Kepler did not, however, abandon the lure of geometry but rather, carried it through with a passion that surpassed even Plato. Driven by the conviction that, in a rational universe, everything must have an explanation, he asked himself why there are only six planets. Immediately, he was struck with the geometric fact that one can only construct five regular solid shapes. If one circumscribed each shape with a circle and placed them within each other, one could construct the ratio's between the various planetary orbits. The universe, then, is a perfectly constructed arrangement of interlocking geometrical forms. Like Copernicus, Kepler's science was rational and not empirical. What was objective was not observational data, which can vary from place to place and observer to observer but, rather, the world of pure mathematical relations. Plato triumphs over Aristotle; what is real is not the messiness of the world of the senses but the pure beauty of mathematical correspondences.

The sun was at the center, the key to the universe; Kepler called the sun "the house of God" and the "heart of the world." From the sun radiates forces which move the planets in the orbits and furnishes the system with energy and balance. Kepler, like Brahe, was convinced of the truth of astrology and made part of his income casting horoscopes and making predictions. The cosmos was one interlocking whole governed by the power of the sun. The constant emanation of light and energy out from the center to diffuse itself through the cosmos -- an image reminiscent of Plotinus, but applied empirically to the sun -- is, for Kepler, a model of God's continual creation.

Thus, there is in Kepler an echo of the alchemical vision of the cosmos as a system of reciprocal forces and powers, and of the

Platonic-Pythagorean dream of a geometrical universe. But there is also something here which neither Plato nor the alchemists would have understood -- the image of the machine. Kepler described his own goal as

> to show that the heavenly machine is not a kind of divine living being but similar to a clockwork in so far as almost all the manifold motions are taken care of by one single absolutely simple magnetic bodily force...and indeed I also show how this physical representation can be presented by calculation and geometrically.

It is said that Kepler wept when he caught the vision of the cosmos as a perfect geometrical form, for he felt he had discovered a secret known only to God. Yet the vision he saw was of a universe perfectly self-contained and explicable by mathematics alone, with no reference to the divine presence.

There is a mysticism in Kepler -- the mysticism of pure mathmatics, the romanticism of ideal inter-relations. In 1619, he published a book entitled <u>The World Harmony</u> in which he probed for even more hidden geometrical relations between the planets, their orbits, velocities, etc. Like the ancient Pythagoreans, he drew an analogy between the relationship among musical tones and the relationships among the planets. He composed scores of the sounds which he thought the planets made in their orbits. What entranced Kepler, however, was the beauty and harmony of the system itself -- little is said of beauty of its source. Kepler was awestruck by the thought of the divine intelligence which fashioned this perfect creation, but what was seen was not the vision of God, but, rather, God's handiwork. In Kepler, astronomy becomes geometry and theology becomes astronomy inspired by awe.

Motivated by a vision of pure mathematical formalism, Kepler showed how heavenly motion could be translated into precise mathematical form. His contemporary, Galileo (1564-1642), applied the same mathematical impetus to motion on earth, and made physics a mathematical science once and for all. Although a convinced Corpernican, Galileo's main contribution involved earthly, not heavenly, motion, In subsuming all movement under a few simple equations, he carried through to its climax the revolution in scientific explanation hinted at by

Copernicus. Aristotle had taught the medieval scientists to account for nature in terms of purpose -- why, for what purpose, does a stone fall or a cart roll down hill? Galileo substituted a new ideal of explanation -- not, for what purpose, but according to what mathematical form do phenomena take place? To explain now means giving a precise mathematical description of what is occurring. The reduction of events to mathematical formula becomes the task of scientific explanation, creating a science called mechanics and banishing teleology forever.

Training the newly-discovered telescope on the heavens, Galileo found a replica of the earth -- bodies in uniform motion according to invariant mathematical principles. Through the telescope, Galileo saw what Kepler theorized -- that the heavens are no different from the earth. Medieval cosmology was at an end. Celestial bodies do not appear unlike earthly ones, nor do they obey different and more divine laws. Nor are thay immutable, for Galileo confirmed what many had claimed before -- that stars and planets came and went (phenomena which today are called nova and comets). Not sacred and transcendent, the heavens are a mechanical system easily grasped by terrestial mathematics. The earth is not the center of the cosmos, but a speck among a multitude of moving bodies. What Aquinas joined together, Galileo put assunder.

Galileo remained throughout his life a loyal Catholic. He considered entering the Jesuits as an adolescent, and, when threatened with the Inquisition, submitted rather than flee as he could have easily done. No doubt Galileo lied when he recanted his belief in the Copernican model, but even after the painful ordeal of the Inquisition, he struggled to balance his scientific convictions with his devotion to the church. But he could only maintain his mechanistic vision and his religious faith by compartmentalizing them. In his <u>Letter to the Grand Duchess Christiana</u> he argued that religion and science are two separate systems of language: The language of mathematics and science -- objective, precise, invariant, and abstract from the passions of everyday life; and the language of religion -- the ordinary language of human feeling, choice, and multiplicity. The one exact, the other less precise; one known only by rigorous effort, the other common to all. The Bible is not a scientific treatise, for it is written "in order to be accommodated to the understanding of every man" and so " is not chained in every expression to conditions as strict as those which govern all physical effects" This theory of two separate disciplines is echoed in his claim of two sources for knowledge of God -- the world as studied through science, and the Bible as received in faith: for "nor is God any less excellently revealed in Nature's actions than in the sacred testaments of the Bible." Only by separating them could the Copernican model and the Biblical narrative be accepted as truth. At the dawn of the science of mechanics, Galileo set the pace for those scientists who wished to remain believers -- they must live with a divided heart.

Medieval theologians generally saw God as the summit of the system -- an Aristotlelian telos towards which everything moved. Galileo's mechanics banished teleology; God can only function at the beginning. Neither the system as a whole, nor its parts, display any purpose other than regular, rigid, and predictable motion. God is the master mathematician and mechamic who invents and constructs the universe which then runs on its own. The beauty of creation points to a God of the past, but not the God of the present. Contemporary intercourse with God has ceased; he remains marvelously apart in both space and time from the universe he created. The medieval world set God above the universe dwelling beyond the crystal sphere, but he continued to direct its course through his secondary agents (particularly men and angels) and occasionally, by a direct, miraculous intervention. All those secondary agents are now swept away; the universe is directed not by angels, but by immanent powers and forces of motion, and God could not intervene to break the regularities he established without contradictiong his own perfect design. The impulse towards transcendence, crystalized in the doctrine of the Trinity, reaches its cosmological climax in the mechanistic universe born from the labor of Copernicus, Kepler, and Galileo.

In France, Galileo's younger contemporary, Rene Descartes (1596-1650) dedicated his life to making a clean break with the past and beginning fresh. Whether such a drastic intellectual housecleaning as Descartes proposed is ever possible is not the question -- Descartes became the ideal of the new philosopher. All authorities were to be questioned; nothing was to be accepted unless proven certain. For all of human history until Descartes and Galileo, time was taken as the test of truth; history and tradition were the surest guides to knowledge; only ideas that had worn well for centuries were trustworthy. Descartes made tradition and antiquity pejorative terms, epithets to be flung at one's opponents, something to be suspected and ridiculed. Descartes, like Plato, was a mathematician who made geometry the essence of Philosophy. Whereas for Plato, aesthetics made geometry the supreme form of wisdom, Descartes was attracted by its absolute demonstrations and invariant relationships. Knowledge worthy of the title must display the certainty of geometric proof; the universe was a system of rigid bodies held together by relationships as invariant as the Pythogorean theorem. Nature fits within a coherent system of mechanical principles, explicable without reference to outside forces.

Descartes was a loyal Catholic who certainly believed in God. Thus he offered proofs for the existence of God which he felt were as certain as the deductions of geometry. The God he argued for is a rational necessity, required to insure the objectivity of the system of correspondence that make up the world and to guarantee that our knowledge of the world is accurate (certainty was Descartes' major compulsion). God created the world by setting up the original conditions of matter and motion, but the universe, like our knowledge of it, once having been set in motion by God, runs on its own. The world and our study of it are both autonomous and comprehensible solely by reason; God fabricates the system according to strict and understandable geometrical principles, then retires.

To allow philosophy and faith to co-exist, Descartes has recourse to the same device as Galileo -- placing God and the human soul outside the boundaries of mechanistic investigation. Descartes' solution was starkly dualistic: Reality contains two completely separate substances -- spirit and matter. Matter is bounded by space and time, exists in fixed shapes, and obeys rigid laws; spirit, mind, or soul is immaterial, occupies no space, is presumably free and not determined, and is immortal. Only in human beings do the spirit and matter co-exist; but, for Descartes they sit side by side with a minimum of interaction. The person is a microcosm of the macrocosm: Like soul and body, God and the physical universe co-exist with a minimum of mutual relationship and influence. Likewise with religion and science -- one the domain of the spirit, the other the domain of matter; intrusions from one field to the other are unnecessary, logically impossible, and a detriment to both. From galaxies down through the human body to the smallest bits of dust, all are composed of rigid bodies undergoing mechanical interactions, separated by an insurmountable logical barrier from the realm of spirit.

In England, Robert Boyle (1627-1691) applied the mechanical outlook to the study of matter: The attributes and alterations of substances resulted from the shape, organization, and activities of component particles. Thus, atomic chemistry was born, a step-child of mechanism. Boyle was one of the most prolific advocates of the mechanistic theory in seventeenth century England; he was also a major Christian thinker who wrote as many pages on theology as on chemistry. Apparently, Boyle experienced a dramatic conversion in his youth, and from henceforth, remained committed to orthodox Christian doctrine and a strict puritan life-style. Boyle never lost sight of the hand of God in the workmanship of creation; the more he investigated the intricacies of matter, the more he was awe-struck by the divine intelligence that must have fashioned such a system, and the more reverent his attitude became towards his maker. The power of God to create such a vast cosmos, the wisdom of God to fashion it so perfectly, the glory of God to interlock all the pieces to run so harmoniously -- these were the pillars of Boyle's nature theology.

To bring together religious and scientific knowledge, Boyle relied on the image used earlier by Galileo -- two books of revelation. In his Usefulness of Experimental Philosophy (1663) he argued that the book of nature is just as much of God's revelation as the Book of Genesis. Beyond that, since nature was made to reveal God's wisdom and glory, God does not wish his message to be ignored. Natural philosophy is a positive religious duty, and the study of nature as much a way of glorifying God as attending services in the parish church. Boyle certainly never intended that one would replace the other, but rather, that both were equally necessary for the religious person in the modern age. As his writings illustrate, Boyle found nature an endless source of pious analogies and lessons on which the faithful could meditate endlessly; disregarding nature was a danger to the soul.

Boyle popularized what was to be the dominate scientific and religious image of the Newtonian epoch -- the clock. Throughout his writings, Boyle alluded to the complex time-keeping mechanism atop the Strasbourg Cathedral. Functioning so smoothly, it appears to be continually guided by an immanent intelligence, but in fact, it is only the mechanical arrangement of parts working together that gives the illusion of continual guidance. Matter is dead and lifeless; it only appears intelligent because, like the pieces of the clock, its components fit together so harmoniously. Such a picture might hardly seem religious at all, but Boyle continually pressed the analogy of the clock into the service of the faith. No one, finding a watch, could imagine that the timepiece constructed itself. Likewise with the cosmos, by no stretch of the imagination could it have created itself. A primal intelligence was necessary to draw up the plans, form the parts, and fit them together. No one has ever seen a watch make itself; all watches are products of the watchmakers' art; likewise, the cosmic mechanism must be the product of the transcendent artisan. The image of the clock conveys the basic principles of Boyle's science and religion: Nature is autonomous, inert, and soul-less, but it reveals the necessity and glory of its Creator in its every movement. By making religion and science pious duties and equal sources of revelation, Boyle held them together theoretically and practically. He could not imagine a time when they would be rent assunder, and men would argue that the contemplation of nature and the book of creation were religion enough, and that churches and Bibles should be done away with; nor beyond that to a time when those who claimed him as their forefather would argue that the watch had, indeed, made itself.

Sir Isaac Newton (1642-1727) took the ideal of mechanical, i.e., mathematical explanation, and applied it to the heavens and made a scientific (in the modern sense) cosmology possible. Kepler described the planetary orbits as elipses, but no mathematical reason could be given for their precise eliptical shape. Galileo had replaced the ancient idea of circular motion with a new absolute -- straight line motion: Bodies in motion stay in motion in a straight line unless disturbed. Newton suggested that the gravitational force from the sun reached out into space and disturbed the natural motion of the planets by drawing them in towards the sun. The combination of these two forces -- momentum moving the planets in a straight line, and solar gravity pulling on them -- would produce an elipse. Soon, more and more celestial and terrestrial phenomena reduced to a few mathematical principles and the ideal of scientific explanation as quantitative description seemed complete. Given the initial conditions of the masses and forces of the system, it would run on like Boyle's beloved clockwork in uniform motion.

Newton, however, rejected the total mechanism of Descartes, refusing to believe that human reason and mechanistic mathematics totally comprehend and explain the universe. As much on the lookout for phenomena that could not be explained mechanically as those that could, he shared little of the impulse of Francis Bacon to use science to dominate nature. Throughout his life, Newton saw science as subservient to piety. "The true calling of science," he wrote in the Optics, "was not to reduce the universe to machine, but to comprehend the system of causality in such a way that it pointed to the First Cause." The Principia was written to prove the existence of God; science exists to serve the divine glory.

Seen through the lens of mechanism, God becomes a functional entity with two major tasks to perform, reflecting Newton's concern to fit the doctrines of creation and providence into a mechanical framework. While forces, like gravity, explain some of the constituents of the universe, they cannot account for its over-all design. That the planets move in the same direction, in nearly concentric orbits around the same sun, that the universe is rational and not random, that there is one sun for heat and light -- all reveal the work of one "very wellskilled in mechanics and geometry". The act of creation means, for Newton, not primarily bringing something into being out of nothing (although Newton did not question creation ex nihilio) but rather, giving it intelligent and harmonious form. Likewise with the doctrine of providence: although Descartes, and even Boyle, felt the world machine was perfect, Newton was not sure; in the Optics, he hinted that the celestial machinery needs retuning from time to time, and that it would even wind down if God did not occasionally intervene and set it right (which earned him Leibniz's taunt that his God was incompetent, for if God were omnipotent, surely he could make a watch that did not need periodic cleaning and repair). However, even if the machine did need occasional repair, Newton's caretaker God, tinkering with the celestial clock, is far from the immediate, personal providence to which Christians had traditionally referred in calling God "Father". God could intervene, but only to save the regularities of the mechanical system.

God stands beyond the world, and oversees it, for he "governs all things, not as the soul of the world, but as Lord over all.... Deity is the dominion of God, not over his own body, as those imagine who fancy God to be the soul of the world, but over servants." Like Boyle's dead clockworks sustaining but the illusion of consciousness, Newton's machine contains no immanent divine intelligence; the image of the potentate God reigns supreme. However, Newton was unhappy with Descartes' total separation of God and matter; he did not want a universe devoid of the presence of God. To affirm both an autonomous mechanical cosmos and the presence of God, Newton drew on an idea popularized by the Cambridge Platonists, that God is infinitely extended in space, and so the universe exists in God. Newton writes in the <u>General Scholium</u> to second edition of the <u>Principia</u>:

> God endures forever and is everywhere present; and, by existing always and everywhere, he constitutes duration and space....In him all things are contained and moved; yet neither affects the other; God suffers nothing from the motion of bodies; bodies find no resistance from the omnipresence of God.

Newton's ambivalence is clear. The universal machine is not devoid of God, for God is "everywhere present" but God's omnipresence affects nothing, and does not interfere with the autonomous motion of the cosmos. God is not immanent within matter, but matter is immanent in God. Newton pushed matter and spirit as close together as mechanism will allow; spirit is present to (not within) matter, but does not compromise its reqularity.

Newton, like Boyle and Galileo before him, made extensive use of the theory of two sources of revelation. Like Galileo, Newton felt that scripture is written in the language of the common man-- "As the Moses, I do not think his description of creation either philosophical or feigned but that he describes realities in a language artificially adaptd to the sense of the vulgar" -- and thus, the Bible is no guide to truth in the literal and precise domain of science. Rather, when approaching the esoteric subject of biblical prophecy to which he devoted considerable time, Newton continually translated the "mystical" imagery into language about ongoing historical events, and then attempted to correlate it with astronomical data in order to arrive at an accurate chronology. There is no doubt that Newton considered the Bible a guide to truth, but the truth it was guide to was moral and historical, not scientific.

While Newton's main focus, both scientifically and theologically, was on astronomy, he did not neglect Boyle's first love -- chemistry. Having compacted the motion of large celestial bodies into succinct mathematical form, he attempted the same for Boyle's corpuscles. Although he never solved the question of intra-atomic forces, he remained convinced that matter, like the solar system, was made of bodies moving according to regular but quasi-mysterious forces. Boyle, while insisting on the existence of atoms, never broke with the major feature of the Aristotelian-medieval chemistry -- the existence of a prima materia, ubiquitous and unchanging. His "atoms" were manifestations of this primal substrata. Newton saw no reason to accept this. In a single long sentence, he decisively shattered the chemistry of his predecessors.

> All things being considered, it seems probable to me that God in the Beginning formed matter in solid, massy, hard, impenetrable, movable Particles, of such sizes and Figures, and with such other Properties and in such Proportion to Space, as most conduced to the end for which He formed them.

For two centuries, the image of "Hard, impenetrable" atoms would reign supreme as scientific orthodoxy.

Throughout the eighteenth and nineteenth centuries, the specification of these particles was the basic task of physics and chemistry. Each had mass, existed in definite numbers, and so were distinct, and were in motion according to Newtonian mechanics. Dalton, early in the nineteenth century, solved the problem of chemical combination by the idea of elementry "atoms" combining in specific

61

proportions. In mid-century, Maxwell described heat in terms of the motion of such elemental pieces of matter. The physical description of atoms, according to Maxwell, fit the chemical description given by Dalton, and from then on the idea of atoms held sway in both physics and chemistry.

Not everything is matter; there is also energy in the form of radiant heat, light, magnetism, and electricity. Maxwell explained the heat of bodies in terms of molecular motion, but radiant heat, the way the sun warms the earth, is obviously not due to any such process. Gradually, it becomes clear that radiant heat is more similar to light than to the temperature of bodies: It can be reflected with a mirror, and refraceted, and it produces interference patterns. In 1800, William Herschel formed a spectrum with a prism and discovery radiant heat at the dark (infra-red) end. Thus, the problem of understanding heat becomes a sub-problem of understanding light.

Newton described light in three ways: a chemical substance (to explain how light affected other substances), mechanical waves, and small particles. The wave theory came to predominate in the nineteenth century for it alone explained the diffraction and interference patterns of light and Foucault's demonstration that light travels slower in water than in air. Yet the image of the waves, drawn from the study of sound, demands a medium through which waves travel - as sound is vibrations of air or ocean waves are ripples of water. If light is a wave, a wave of what? Such waves would have to be propagated in a medium (Newton called it ether) in space that is both extremely elastic, and yet dense. No conceivable substance could be dense enough to propagate waves and yet not retard the motion of the planets as they passed through it.

Throughout the nineteenth century, Faraday and Maxwell worked on understanding electricity and magnetism. Faraday's pragmatic and pictoral experiments uncovered many of the formerly mysterious aspects of these phenomena which Maxwell transcribed into complex mathematical formulas. Maxwell's equations for electric and magnetic fields turned out to have the form of wave equations, the same form found in equations describing the intensity of light. Beyond that, Maxwell's equations contained a constant just as those for light waves did. Maxwell calculated the magnitude of his "electric constant", and found it to be the speed of light, the constant of the light wave equations.

The sudden congruence of Maxwell's equations for electricity and magnetism with the equations for light waves lead to the obvious conclusion -- both are functions of the same type of waves. But again, waves in what? Maxwell remained a Newtonian, firmly believing that waves must be propagated through a medium, and developed a complex theory of what this ether must be like to support the waves we call light, electricity, and magnetism. Even energy (propagated in waves) is seen in a quasi-materialistic and mechanical way. While not a material substance, energy propagates mechanically through a material medium. Maxwell's equations reinforced the movement of physics that began with Newton's Principia. When Maxwell wrote his own account of the current state of physics, he called it Matter in Motion, a title which reveals the basic thrust of Newtonian physics -- everything can be explained in terms of the motion of material entities. Light, electricity, and magnetism, as well as falling bodies, planetary motion, and the behavior of gas are all the result of billiard balls moving through space. Lord Kelvin, who remained skeptical of Maxwell's elaborate theory of ether, spoke for the same ideal when he wrote, "I can never satisfy myself until I can make a mechanical model of a thing. If I can make a mechanical model, I can understand it."

The Religion of Nature or the Nature of Religion

The generation of Boyle and Newton intimately connected religion and science; neither experimenter could write a treatise on planetary motion or chemical compositon without mentioning God. Rational investigation was the handmaiden of piety; through studying nature, nature's creator would be found. The deity found there, however, is far from the Heavenly Father of traditional faith. Boyle and Newton fought hard to keep together two distinct images of God: the loving, providential father and the omnipotent geometer: One image inherited from the past, the other pointing towards the future.

The next generation found the battle not worth fighting. Younger contemporaries and those coming to maturity in the eighteenth century saw no reason to keep the mantle of Christianity inwhich the seventeenth century Chrisitan virtuosi had garbed the God of nature. At the turn of the century, John Toland (1670-1722) published <u>Christianity Not Mysterious</u>, premised on the conviction that "Reason is the only Foundation of all Certitude; and nothing reveal'd....is more exempted from its Disquisitions than the ordinary Phenomena of Nature." While evaluating religion by the methods proving so fruitful in clearing away the mysteries of the planetary system, Toland was far from an atheist or an anti-Christian polemicist. His aim in writing was to show "that there is nothing in the Gospel contrary to Reason." We cannot believe anything, Toland argued, unless we understand what it is we are assenting to, and we cannot understand something unless we can form a conception of it. Notions of which we can form no clear conception are simply nonsense, and "say just nothing." "What I don't conceive," Toland wrote " can no more give me right Notions of God, or influence my Actions, than a Prayer deliver'd in an unknown Tongue can excite my Devotion." The basic gospel is perfectly reasonable and comprehensible to "what we call Common Sense." The so-called mysterious elements in Christianity were creatd by religious officials who sought to maintain their own monopoly on the truth by hiding the rational core of Christianity behind a smoke-screen of creeds, liturgies, and traditions.

Toland's essay thrusts against the importance of revelation; we can know the truth about God from nature, since " the very Supposition that Reason might authorize one thing, and the Spirit of God another, throws us into inevitable Scepticism." Little is said about the nature of God, but it is clear that Toland's deity is the master craftsman of the world mechanism whose chief attribute is his capacity to fashion the harmonious planetary machine. This alone is rational; revelation is superfluous for "the New Testament....must consequently agree with Natural Reason and our own ordinary Ideas." Toland's book brought forth more than a hundred angry replies, and was ordered publicly burned by the Irish House of Commons.

The same argument was continued in a polemic by Matthew Tindal (1657-1733) appropriately entitled, <u>Christianity as Old as Creation</u> (1733) by asserting that the essential religion is that of the First Cause known through nature; revealed religion is unnecessary, if not pernicious. The highest glory that can be given to God is to appreciate his perfect ordering of the system of nature. Science, which uncovers these splendid regularities, is more authentically religious than traditions about revelation which obscure them. Not willing to break completely with the past, Tindal called himself a "Christian Deist."

The same points were being made on the continent by Gotthold Lessing (1729-1781) who published a series of attacks on the historicity of the Bible. There was one universal religion, Lessing argued, but "out of the religion of nature, which was not capable of being universally practiced by all men alike, a positive religion had to be constructed." But now, through the evolution of man's rational abilities, we can enjoy that pure, natural religion once more, and can dispense with the particular religious traditions which were its carriers. Wrote Lessing:

> The Bible obviously contains more than is essential to religion. Religion was there before the Bible existed. Christianity was there before the evangelists and apostles wrote.

Apostles and prophets are to be judged by the rationality of their claims for "the religion is not true because the evangelists and apostles taught it; but they taught it because it is true." The attack climaxed at the end of the century in the verbal musket fire of Thomas Paine's (1737-1809) <u>Age of Reason</u>. Having rejected revelation as a "pious fraud" which is "useless and unnecessary", Paine asserted, "The Word of God is The creation We Behold: And it is in this word, which no human being can counterfeit or alter, that God speaketh universally to man." Thus Paine insisted, "It is only by the exercise of reason that man can discover God" and the only God there is to discover is "that of a first cause, the cause of all things." Paine is not without his piety; he can declaim as eloquently as Boyle or Newton on the splendor of God in creation.

> Do we want to contemplate his power? We see it in the immensity of creation. Do we want to contemplate his wisdom? We see it in the unchangeable order by which the incomprehensible whole is governed. Do we want to contemplate his

munificence? We see it in the abundance with which he fills the earth....Search not the book called the scripture, which any human hand might make, but the book called the Creation.

Revelations and texts are always second-hand; God can be met directly through his celestial handiwork.

Newton and Boyle, like Copernicus and Kepler before them, were awestruck by the discovery which today is taken for granted--that the universe is comprehensible by human reason; that mankind can understand the cosmos! Such a forceful realization had the quality of mystical ecstasy: "The delight I took in my discovery," Kepler wrote, "I shall never be able to describe in words." Newton and Boyle were content to lose themselves in wonder. In the eighteenth centyry, awe turned to anger, and the book of nature struck against the Bible. The bulk of the tracts written by the proponents of the religion of nature were not pious calls to rise to a vision of the first cause by mediating on the splendors of the celestial harmony, but vitriolic assaults on religious tradition in the name of the democracy of reason. The impulse in the religion of nature was to reduce everything to a state of rational consiousness. Mystery, liturgy, symbolism are out. Nature and piety both must be measured by a fanatical, mechanical literalness. The mechanical myth -- enshrined in the worship of "common sense" -- was the only guide to truth.

Deists were, however, religious men, worshipping their God in the way most congruent with the deity they believed in, by being intent upon moral rectitude in public and private affairs. Throughout their writings, the image of the will predominates. God is the paramount cosmic volition, whose rationally guided choices are supremely displayed in nature. Human response to God is, likewise, rational choice, to pursue the investigation of nature, to seek truth, to live uprightly. Throughout the eighteenth century, God gradually drops out of treatises on physics and chemistry, but remains central in essays on ethics.

Mechanism killed nature, rendering it dead atoms, grooved into unspontaneous orbits. One way to keep God from dying too was to remove him far beyond the watchmaker's cosmos. In time and space, God was totally separate from the rigidities of invariant motion, bound to his creation only by a single, prehistoric act of will. The enticements of natural explanation were sufficiently enthralling to capture the human fancy. A distant god paled in comparison to increasing theoretical synthesis and technical ingenuity; by the end of the eigthteenth century, they completely filled or restricted the field of consciousness. What Boyle and Newton took as nourishment for piety pushed religion as far beyond the scope of human concern as the deist's God was beyond the unniverse of his contrivance.

The Moral Imperative

By the end of the eighteenth century, new and more skeptical voices were being heard from the wings. In 1776, David Hume (1711-1776) published his <u>Dialogues Concerning Natural Religion</u>. Deism had turned the religion of reason against the revealed religion from which it sprung, Hume turned reason against the religion of reason which had carried the rationalist imperative for most of the century. In brief, Hume drew on the tradition going back at least to Francis Bacon, that knowledge is based on experience, but, he added we have no experience of such things as causality. Causality is an inference we draw in order to make sense of our experiences; it is not something we can prove with the certainty Descartes demands. Causality is a useful tool, not the metaphysical key to the cosmos. Without the key, the door remains locked; there can be no argument for a first cause, for there is no way to establish the principle of causality with which the argument begins. Although Hume mentioned in his dialogues that skepticism can lead to faith, the result of his skepticism about the use of reason in a religious matters meant a hasty demise of the religion of reason. Deism was a transitional phenomena, carrying forward the mechanistic imperative under the guise of a religious impulse. When the religion of reason itself became, after Hume, irrational, it died from self-contradiction, leaving mechanistic reason to develop on its own. Its only relation to religion, which had given it birth and carried it forward, was one of relentless conflict.

In Immanuel Kant (1725-1804) the seed which Galileo had planted became a full-grown and sturdy tree, and the drive to separate religion and reason found systematic and rigorous expression. Kant's German, pietistic upbringing would not let him dispense with Christianity entirely, nor would his scientific inclinations let him be content with Hume's skepticism. Seeking to save both scientific reason and religious faith from Hume's onslaught, he hit on a schema which he could only compare with Copernicus' revolution. Granted that we do not experience directly such fundamental physical categories as causality, space, time, Kant said, that does not make them specious. These categories (to use his word) are rooted in our mind, and presumably, therefore grounded in reality. We can only experience the world in terms of these categories because they represent the fundamental structures of our thinking. We can no more conceive of the world in terms other than causality than we can conceive of a square circle. Through the structure of the mind, science is rooted in reality.

Reason functions only in conjunction with data from the physical world. Kant agreed with Hume: There can be no rational proofs for the existence of God; the cord that Newton and Boyle (and the Deists) used to join religion and science was forever cut. There is no way to start with nature and argue to God, for reason is condemned to labor within the prison of finitude. Morality, however, remains in the domain of rationality. What such "practical reason" demonstrates is the necessity of acting with a universal conscience and not doing any act one would not want generalized to all. God sustains this moral law as the sovereign judge who will insure that, in the next life, the righteous are duly rewarded. The rigidity of the just moral law, matching the invariant laws of nature, the freedom to act, and an immortal state in which justice can triumph -- these postulates require God's existence.

In 1793, Kant published <u>Religion Within the Limits of Reason Alone</u>, in which he delineated the role of religion in the world created by man's mechanistic and finite consciousness. There can be no intercourse between the infinite God and this finite world; Kant's God is as distant from the universe as that of the Deists. God exists not to guarantee the workings of nature -- Kant's mechanism surpasses Newton's; nature now runs totally on its own -- but the workings of morality. The religious imperative is not "to think God's thoughts after Him," for that is now impossible, but to act rightly within the sphere of finitude. Shorn of any possible religious significance, science travels its road alone. Religion only exists to inculcate the duty of moral obedience; it can say nothing about the physical world. Science and religion now live on, each secure in a splendid autonomy, with no conceivable interaction between them.

In the work of Albrecht Ritschl (1822-1889), the Kantian solution to the relation of religion and science, God and nature, is developed into a complete theology. Ritschl predicated his massive work, <u>The Christian Doctrine of Justification and Reconciliation</u> (1870) on a distinction between judgments of fact and judgments of value. Judgments of fact, the domain of science, are disinterested, objective, and universal; they concern the world as a whole; they do not concern us personally as unique individuals. Judgments of value, the domain of religion, express what is of utmost value to each of us as a person. Religion and science belong to utterly different modes of consciousness: one detached and antiseptic; one passionate and involved. Although a person can be both a scientist and a believer (and one should be both for both modes are part of the fullness of human consciousness), it would seem one could not be both at the same time. Signifying different cognitive styles, religion and science also represent different objects. Religion attends to the personal world of value where choices are freely made; science to the impersonal world of nature where bodies move predictably. Descartes' separation of matter and spirit has now hardened into a distinction between two distinct disciplines, with opposing objects of study -- matter cannot be understood spiritually, nor can spirit be investigated scientifically.

Paralleling the separation of religion and science, Ritschl compartmentalizes God and the world. Ritschl's uncompromising negation of any meeting point between the transcendent God and the finite world is expressed as a tireless polemic against what he calls mysticism. Even in human consciousness -- which Descartes hinted might contain some interaction of spirit and matter -- there is no meeting place of the finite and the infinite. The early mechanists explicitly rejected the image of a world soul, but retained an element of infinity in the human soul.

Relentless Kantian that he is, Ritschl sees human nature totally engulfed in finitude. There can be no divine immanence, no presence of spirit within man or matter. The landscape painted by Kant and Ritschl is as cold and bleak as the surface of the moon first appearing in Galileo's telescope. To man's finite eyes, the heavens can no longer declare the glory of God, nor can his finite ears catch the strains of the harmony of the spheres. The divine spirit is no longer perceived as the matrix in which all motion takes place; there is only dead matter swirling in purposeless orbits. The mind no longer rises up in joyful contemplation of the first cause; it only picks its way among disconnected fragments, arbitrarily fitted into some theoretical mold. Caught in a ceaseless struggle between right and wrong, mankind trudges across this desolate stage, weighed down by the burden of unrelieved moral obligation. Boyle and Newton could not have recognized this as the outcome of their sanctified science.

This is not to say that Ritschl is uninfluenced by science, rather, his whole definition of the human enterprise fulfills the tendencies of Bacon and Descartes. To Ritschl, the goal of human existence is mastery of the world, the imposition of the human will onto a dead and plastic matter. His primary impulse is to take charge. For Ritschl, society and culture are as much a part of nature as is the physical world; ethics represents the mastery of the cultural world in a way analogous to technology's control of nature. Christianity, he argued, is not world denying, but world mastering; its primary imperative is to take control of man's cultural life and shape it into the kingdom of God. Religious ethics becomes a form of technology; Jesus supplies the blueprint and inspiration with which the technician of morality works. Religion is a duty, to alter the world morally, as science is altering the world physically. Religion and science work in separate compartments, but they perform analogous tasks.

The Recovery of Presence

The eventual hegemony of mechanical reason set the agenda for western religion in the eighteenth and nineteenth centuries. Now religion was on the defensive. The perplexing question was no longer how could Copernicus' planetary orbits and Galileo's observations fit in with the world as God created it, but, rather, how could God fit into the world that Descartes, Newton, and Maxwell had created? Having extracted a submission from Galileo, theology was suddenly standing before the bar of reason and being found wanting. God had to find a place in the mechanistic universe or be discarded altogether; religion had to find a haven in the modern world, safe from critical attack.

No doubt these questions were on the mind of the greatest nineteenth century theologian, Friedrich Schleiermacher (1768-1834) and his artfully sculptured systematic theology The Christian Faith (1821) can be read as his answer. Schleiermacher began with a general definition of religion as a form of self-consciousness. Breaking with the definitional dominance of Kant, for Schleiermacher, the domain of religion is not ethics, but emotion; it is "neither a Knowing or a Doing but a modification of Feeling, or of immediate self-consciousness". Neither ethics ("doing") nor science ("knowing"), religion concerns the way in which the self becomes aware of itself; religion is the most primal and searching form of introspection. As I become conscious of myself as a person, Schleiermacher argued, my most primary awareness is that I did not create myself. Our primal sensation is "the consciousness of being absolutely dependent" -- that is, that we did not create ourselves -- which, Schleiermacher said, is the same as the consciousness, "of being in relation with God".

At the very outset, Schleiermacher insisted that theology is to borrow no propositions from science or ethics, but to confine itself only to statements about its particular subject matter -- the awareness of absolute dependence. Newton's mechanism and Kant's critiques had robbed science of any theological usefulness. In Schleiermacher's own time, the rise of critical history, based on mechanical reason, was turning its artillary on the bible with results more devastating than the attacks of the Deists. Schleiermacher was also aware that agnostic systems of philosophy and ethics, drawing on reason alone, were being created in the classrooms of England and the continent. Beginning with science, the modern world was steadily depriving theology of its handmaidens and supporters: first science, then philosophy, and now history and ethics were being swept away by the advancing mechanical empire. Supports for faith, once anchored in nature, reason, or history, were crumbling. By grounding religion in immediate experience -- one area seemingly immune from critical attack -- Schleiermacher no doubt felt he had found a secure foundation; he could not foresee Sigmund Freud, born twenty years after Schleiermacher's death, who extended the image of the machine into the depths of human consciousness.

God represesents the unknown "whence" behind our awareness of absolute dependence; God is the term we use to signify the fact that we did not create ourselves. At its root, the term "God" refers not to what actually gives rise to our existence -- that, after all, would be a statement about physical and biological processes which lie outside the domain of religion -- but only to the _feeling_ that we are not self-generating but depend on something beyond our control for the giveness of our existence. Piety, then, is not separate from the world but is, rather, a way of perceiving the world in which "we place all that affects or influences us in absolute dependence upon God." Schleiermacher accepted that "all things are conditioned and determined by the interdependence of Nature." Nothing exists outside of mechanical causality. His response, however, was just the reverse of the stark dualism of Descartes and the Deists. Rather than separating God's action from the processes of nature, Shcleiermacher made them coincide. To be religious means to perceive the action of God coming to us in and through the determinacies of nature. "In each and every situation," Schleiermacher wrote, "we ought to be conscious of, and sympathetically experience, absolute dependence upon God just as we conceive of each and every thing as completely conditioned by the interdependence of nature."

Later, polemically inclined, commentators saw in Schleiermacher's words the spectre of pantheism but it is quite clear that he does not identify God with the system of nature, nor God's action with natural causation. Schleiermacher's rigid demarcation of the domain of theology and stringency in keeping it distinct from science and philosophy insure that statements about natural causation, belonging to science, have no place in theology which can speak only about the contents of self-consciousness. Observing the same natural system, the scientist sees mechanical regularities and the believer sees divine action. Statements about God and statements about nature are two entirely different types of language and cannot be equated.

Logically, God and world belong to different classes but practically they cannot be separated. Piety, then, is developed not by fleeing the world but by immersing oneself in it, for piety "is most complete when we identify ourselves in our self-consciousness with the whole world." God is not another term for the cosmos but it is only through the cosmos that God is present to us. Reversing the main theological impulse governing the relation of God and the world since the council of Nicaea, Schleiermacher understands God's action in terms of immanence, not transcendence. God comes to us in and through the material mechanisms of the universe; to be governed by God is coterminous with being governed by the laws of nature. "The absolute dependence of all events and changes on God," Schleiermacher wrote, "and natural causation...are one and the same thing, simply from different points of view."

In a mechanistic universe, the majority of theologians in the eighteenth and nineteenth centuries could find a place for God only by removing him as far as possible from the celestial machinery. Making the opposite response, Schleiermacher, while continuing the now-traditional compartmentalization of religion and science, homogenizes God's will and nature's causation. For both, conflict between God's action and natural laws is eliminated: For the Deists, God no longer acts,; for Schleiermacher, he only acts in and through physical regularities. Whereas the mainstream theological emphasis is on distance, Schleiermacher's impulse is towards God's presence but in a way that does not contradict the dominance of the machine.

While nearly identifying God's presence with the processes of nature, Schleiermacher felt no need to give a theological description of the physical world. Such an account is explicitly ruled out by his strict allegiance to the separation of religion and science. Even statements about the doctrine of creation are statements about God (or, more precisely, our awareness of God coming through the world), not statements about the constitution of physical or biological reality. Schleiermacher's universe is still mechanical but it is not the barren and moralistic universe of Kant and Ritschl. It is a universe romantically infused with feeling and warm with the presence of God but also mechanistic and deterministic: thus intensifying the divided heart and mind which, from Galileo onward, lived within the scientifically sophisticated theologian and the religiously sensitive scientist. Finding the starkness of Cartesian and Kantian mechanism narrow and unrealistic, while forced to subscribe to the Newtonian paradigm, left Schleiermacher no other choice but to inhabit two totally different and mutually exclusive worlds. Such intellectual schizophernia is hard to sustain. No wonder that few were able to maintain both Schleiermacher's ecstatic devotion and also a commitment to the world. Throughout the nineteenth and early twentieth centuries, fervent piety tended to remain in those who withdrew from the world and its sciences into evangelical sectarianism, and those who continued to "identify themselves with the whole world" tended to be abstractly philosophical, like the followers of Hegel, or rigidly moralistic like the followers of Ritschl, both of whom condemn Schleiermacher for his "mysticism."

The Triumph of Separation

Kepler's ecstasy at discovering that the heavens could be comprehended by human reason set the tone for the following three hundred years. If reason could storm the heavens, it must be the only guide to truth. Such contagious excitement at human powers spread through the seventeenth and eighteenth centuries, infecting the western mind with a degree of optimism never before experienced. The nineteenth century added Darwin's theory of evolution and, although Darwin's Origin of the Species extended the impersonal mechanistic empire into the realm of biology, in the popular mind, evolution never lost its progressivistic and teleological connotations. Through the natural unfolding of rational discovery, mankind was inexorably moving forward; utopia was within reach.

All of this came to a brutal end in the trenches of World War One. It is hard to over-estimate the fracturing impact of the war: Ideals of human brotherhood shattered by artillary fire; inevitable progress derailed by inconceivable savagery on the part of those nations considered most civilized; even science called into question by its production of undreamed-of weapons of mass murder. Optimistic and humanistic platitudes no longer rang true. The era of disillusionment expressed itself philosophically and artistically in the essays and plays of existentialism -- coercing western eyes to contemplate the limits of human nature, the inevitability of suffering and death, the futility of choice, the meaninglessness of life in a random and uncaring mechanistic universe. The religious counterpart was a vigorous return to tradition. Combining the imagery of existentialism with the language of the Bible, such neo-orthodox leaders as Karl Barth (1886-1968) and Paul Tillich (1886-1965) powerfully re-declared the themes of human sinfulness and divine sovereignty, lost in the moralism and humanism of nineteenth century theology. Sermons on God's judgment and man's sin were heard gladly in an age forced to rediscover human finitude while culture crumbled.

Twentieth century theology began with a post-war attempt to repudiate the major tenets of the nineteenth century, but the repudiation was carried on in the categories forged by the very people being rejected. Barth used Kant's prison of finitude to insist that man is uncompromisingly finite; human reason cannot reach God. This thoroughly Kantian anthropology leaves mankind totally dependent upon God's revelation for any knowledge of God. Revelation, for Barth, is the essence of Christianiy, but it is understood in compartmentalized terms that Kant, Ritschl, and Schleiermacher would have understood. For Barth, revelation affects only the relation between God and the individual; it says nothing about science, philosophy, or reason. Barth never tired of pounding home the message that the attempt to understand "religion within the limits of reason alone" was the unforgiveable sin of his forefathers. God and the life of faith are totally beyond the small circle of human finitude. "What is pleasing to god," Barth wrote in his theological <u>Commentary</u> on <u>Paul's Letter to the Romans</u>, the book which halted the whole nineteenth century theological enterprise, "comes into being when all human righteousness is gone, irretrievably gone, when men are uncertain and lost, when they have abandoned all ethical and religious illusions, and when they have renounced every hope in this world and in heaven." Powerful medicine, given as an antidote to the corporate ego-mania of the nineteenth century.

Science, philosophy, even religion, are totally finite human enterprises which say nothing about the nature of God or the experience of faith. In using Kant to criticize Kant, Barth did not acknowledge that his setting faith free from any rational and empirical constraints continued the basic thrust of nineteenth century theology -- the imprisoning of faith in its own, private, intellectual cell.

Barth asserted the tradition of divine transcendence with a Kantian vengeance. Having reduced every created thing to abject finitude, there is no place for God but totally beyond creation. Barth wrote:

> God is not a particular instance within a class. When we Christians speak of 'God', we may and must be clear that this word signifies a <u>priori</u> the fundamentally Other, the fundamental deliverance from the whole world of man's seeking, conjecturing, illusion, imagining, and speculating.... He is the One who stands <u>above</u> us and also above our highest and deepest feelings, strivings, intuitions, above the products, even the most sublime, of the human spirit.

There can be no meeting place between creator and creature; Barth continually reiterated Kierkegaard's image of an "infinite qualitative difference between man and God", and if God is totally distinct from man, he is even more distinct from the physical creation. In his free and sovereign will, God has chosen to bind himself to creation in a covenant of love, but, in Barth's typically paradoxical style, even in binding himself to the world, God remains free, even in being present to mankind in revelation God remains hidden. God's radical <u>otherness</u> is the essence of deity, and can never be compromised.

Barth recovered the mainstream tradition going back to the council of Nicaea--God's divinity is his transcendence over the physical world -- and builds an imposing and thoroughly consistent dogmatic edifice on that single corner-stone. By being both more constructive and more rooted in tradition, Barth is probably a greater theologian than his nemesis Schleiermacher, but his solution to the problem of God and the world, religion and science, is but a more extreme version of Scheiermacher's. Barth so compartmentalizes faith that science is totally irrelevant. The power of Barth's vision comes in part from his relentless insistence on the integrity of the theological task: Religious spokespersons need not seek the approval of the scientist or the philospher, nor should they, for they have an urgent task that is theirs alone -- bringing mankind into relationship with God. Science and philosophy, bound to the categories of finitude, cannot assess this transcendental relationship, and must lapse into silence before God's self-revelation. Such a freedom comes at a penalty. Liberated from the constraints of mechanistic and reductionistic science, the theologian is entrapped in his own theological circle. To speak of the world theologically is a contradiction in terms; for Barth (as for Schleiermacher, and even Ritschl) theology speaks only of God. To do otherwise is to compromise the crystalline purity of the theological task.

Paul Tillich, like Barth, lost his optimism on the battlefields of Europe. Working more in the spirit of Schleiermacher's <u>Christian Faith</u> and Hegel's <u>Phenomenology</u> than Kant's <u>Critique</u>, Tillich drove toward synthesis rather than the stringent compartmentalization of Barth. Defining religion as the depth dimension of culture gave Tillich an openness to the world and propeled him to write a series of essays on "religion and..." -- religion and politics, religion and art, religion and psychoanalysis. Tillich's God is the "Ground of Being" -- the primal source of existence, the underlying structure of reality -- again an image of immanence closer to Schleiermacher than to Barth. God is that "power of being" standing between the world and its non-existence. Since the term "God" is intimately bound to images of "being", "existence", "reality", creation is the fundamental doctrine of divinity. "The divine life and the divine creativity are not different," Tillich wrote, "God is creative because he is God....The doctrine of creation is not the story of an event which took place 'once upon a time', it is the basic description of the relation between God and the world." Universal generativity rather than absolute transcendence marks the essence of divinity.

This ontologizing of creation binds God and the world together. Since there is no difference in God between potentiality and actuality, creation is necessary for God is necessarily creative; in order for God to be God, there must be an object of his creative potency. And if God is eternal, it would seem creation must also be eternal; Origen, Aquinas, and Schleiermacher had reasoned the same. However, the most fundamental fact about creation, for Tillich, is its finitude -- here is his debt to Kant and existentialism and his affinity for Barth. By definition, the created order is finite, contingent, particular, and transitory; God alone is universal and necessary. Put slightly differently, "creation" refers to the particular and contingent elements of the system of reality; "God" refers to the one, universal and necessary element. Creation exists in unresolved tension represented by three "ontological polarities": individualization and participation (the particular and the universal); dynamics and form (change and continuity); freedom and destiny (choice and determinism). In constant oscillation between these polarities and continually under the threat of non-being, finite creation has no possibility of peace and harmony within itself, and so "points beyond itself" to its divine ground. In reunion with its source, mankind stills the warfare of unresolved polarities in the experience Tillich called "the new being" and overcomes the threat posed by presence of non-being by the act of "ontological courage." Possible even within finitude, these experiences point to the eschaton, the "non-fragmentary, total, complete conquest of the ambiguities of life." What of creation apart from man: Tillich refused to speculate on what "eternal blessedness means for the universe besides man," calling such concerns "poetic-symbolic." While deeply in Origen's debt, Tillich steered clear of the image of "apocatastasis."

While the category of creation is central to his doctrine of God, Tillich steadfastly refused to attempt a theological understanding of the physical world. Despite his boundless openness to the social and intellectual currents of the modern age -- more openness than was displayed by any other Christian theologian of the first half of this century -- there is one "religion and ..." essay that Tillich never wrote: Religion and natural science. (A paper by that title in <u>Theology of Culture</u> really discussed only the idea of a personal God.) No less than Kant, Schleiermacher, or Barth, Tillich continued the defensive search for the unique and transcendental essence of religion and the most secure way to wall it off from critical assault. What Kant found in ethics, Schleiermacher in self-consciousness, Barth in personal revelation, Tillich found in the experiential awareness that one's particular individuality is grounded in the universal power of being -- a state of consciousness variously called "the new being", "being grasped by the unconditional", "ultimate concern", and simply "faith". In his impressively popular little book, <u>The Dynamics of Faith</u> and his collections of sermons <u>The New Being</u> and <u>The Shaking of the Foundations</u> (all so down-to-earth and stirring that it's hard to believe they were preached by the author of <u>The Systematic Theology</u>), Tillich makes it clear that religious faith has nothing to do with scientific-like claims about the universe. Faith is one state of consciousness, and all it can lay claim to (a'la Schleiermacher) is statements about its unique form of awareness of the universal. Thus, Tillich clearly asserts that "scientific truth and the truth of faith do not belong to the same dimension of meaning. Science has no right and no power to interfere with faith and faith has no power to interfere with science. One dimension of meaning is not able to interfere with another dimension.... Science can only conflict with science and faith only with faith." The defensive tone of Tillich's compartmentalization is clear from the phrases that highlight his discussion of religion and science -- "no right and no power to interfere," "its own valid dimension," "conflict." The laudable goal of insuring there are no more inquisitions of would-be Galileo's or misguided polemics by future Tom Paines comes at the cost of never being able to produce a unified view of the world.

<u>The Defensive Offensive</u>
Throughout the eighteenth and nineteenth centuries, the mechanistic empire brought more and more territory under its materialistic and reductionistic hegemony. Everywhere investigators went, they listened only for the hum of machinery. Darwin applied the same model to the origin of the human species, and, in the most daring move of all, Sigmund Freud brought even the human psyche under the domination of the machine. The intellectual-social territory of religion shrank proportionately to the advance of the machine; the cold, hard whirling billiard balls of matter left no room for the spirit of God or man, the rigid invariances of mathematical motion left no place for human or divine initiative.

The grand cosmological visions of the fathers were reduced to quibbling about moral rules or states of consciousness. Descartes, Boyle, and Newton agreed that mechanism meant that matter was dead -- its movements only apparently purposeful, like the ticking of a well-wrought clock -- but within the human personality, and around the purring cosmos, dwelt a living and choosing spirit. By the time Darwin died and Freud started writing, all reality lay dead. Spirit vanquished; matter in motion ruled supreme.

The defensive posture of theology in the modern world is clear in the compartmentalization embraced by Kant, Ritschl, Scheiermacher, Barth, and Tillich. On the defensive long enough, communities will take to the offense. In ways that horrified the more irenic intellectuals of the nineteenth century, the community of faith again took the offensive against science. In 1864, Pope Pius IX issued his encyclical <u>The Syllabus of Errors</u>; among the errors condemned were the denial of the "action of God upon man and the world", that "human reason....is the sole arbiter of truth", that "Divine revelation is imperfect", and lastly, that "The Roman Pontiff can and ought to reconcile himself to....progress, liberalism, and civilization." This was followed at the beginning of the twentieth century by another list of condemned propositions, penned by Pope Pius X. Among those anathamatized were that "the church has no right to pass judgment on the human sciences," that "Divine inspiration does not extend to all of Sacred Scriptures;" that "Scientific progress demands that concepts of Christian doctrine concerning God, creation....be re-adjusted," and that "Catholicism can be reconciled with true science only if it is transformed into a non-dogmatic Christianity; that is to say, into a broad and liberal Protestantism." Battle lines were drawn up again.

In a similar mood, two wealthy American conservative Protestants arranged for the publication of a series of pamphlets in 1909 entitled the <u>Fundamentals</u>, in which the conservative Protestant stand on the issues of the day was articulated. While the pamphlets were basically moderate in tone and reasonably argued, it is clear that science is an object of suspicion. The suspicion fanned the fires of a crusaded that sent evangelical armies into state legislatures throughout the country to lobby for laws against teaching scientific theories in the public schools which contradicted Biblical accounts of cosmic and human genesis. The crusade surfaced into public view in July of 1925, when John Scopes was put on trial in Dayton, Tennessee for teaching Darwin's theory of evolution.

To the Catholic hierarchy and the conservative Protestant of the early twentieth century, it is clear that science and religion do not inhabit different worlds, and that a unified view of the world is necessary to both religion and science. Although commonly accused of irrationality, the conservatives saw themselves as defenders of reason, for it seemed contradictory to the coherence of truth that reality should be split into antagonistic compartments. Ironically, though, the conservative attack on modernism was powered by a narrowly modern model of truth -- that mechanical, literal, empirical statements are the essence of reality. Thus, in their attempt to force a unitary outlook on the world, the conservatives compelled religion and science to fight over the same small narrow band of truth -- the literal description of empirical events. Since truth had to be deadeningly literal, science had to agree with the literalness of the Genesis account as understood on the model of Newton's __Principia__ as earlier religion had to submit to the literalness of Maxwell's __Matter in Motion__. Because the base on which both the fans of Clarence Darrow and the supporters of William Jennings Bryan built their respective cases was so narrow, no compromise was possible and the battle of the literalists has dragged on to this day.

From whatever tradition he or she came, most Christians coming to maturity in the middle of the twentieth century could be assured that natural science was, at best, irrelevant, and at worst, demonic. Beyond that, the tradition of the fathers in attempting to understand the universe theologically was clearly misguided or even superstitious and heretical. Either the Biblical account was enough, and so science was unnecessary for piety, or the scientific account was logically pursuasive but religiously extraneous. To the conservative, science was an enemy to be subdued; to the neo-orthodox, the scientist was a colleague to be ignored. To the mainstream of theological thought, it was enough to say God created the world without implying any understanding of the world God created. God and the universe, religion and science, moved along in separate compartments reminiscent of Descartes' non-mingling spirit and matter. Such was modern theology's inheritance from the myth of the machine.

CHAPTER FIVE:

THE DEMISE OF THE MACHINE

The Shattering of Matter

At the turn of the century, the grip of mechanism began to loosen; the parts of its empire went into revolt. In the nineteenth century, physicists had known that an electric current passed between two plates in an empty tube gives off rays; these were thought to be another form of electro-magnetic radiation. By the year nineteen hundred, J. J. Thomson had proven they were not; rather, they were a stream of tiny, tiny particles (with mass less than a thousandth of a hydrogen atom) carrying a negative electrical charge. Thomson resisted his conclusions. The more he experimented, the more he was forced to accept that the basis of the physical world was not solid billiard balls of matter but particles many times smaller and the basis of chemical elements was not a specific atom unique to each but more primary particles shared in common by all elements: Chemical elements were no longer elemental. So offensive was this discovery that Thomson was accused of playing a practical joke; his results were ridiculed. At the same time, the Curies, experimenting with radioactivity, discovered that the apparently immutable elements of classical chemistry changed. As the heavier elements (like radium) gave off radioactivity, they turned into lead. And the radioactivity they gave off was in the form of particles like those Thomson proposed.

While the foundation of the early atomic idea was being shaken, the same thing was happening to the idea of energy as mechanical waves. Waves travel smoothly through a medium, theoretically almost any frequency of a wave is possible -- any pitch of sound or rate of ocean waves. In 1899, Max Planck argued that light was not absorbed or emitted in continuous frequencies but in discrete packets or quanta. The size of the quanta was proportional to the frequency of the wave. While enabling scientists to account for radiation under certain conditions, such a concept made no sense. Everyone knew that waves were not packets. In 1905, Albert Einstein carried Planck's suggestion to its logical conclusion: Light and other forms of electro-magnetic radiation are not only absorbed in packets; they exist in packets as well. Electro-magnetic radiation (including light) travels in waves, but the waves consist of packets called photons. Each photon is, in essence, a kind of particle which strikes a surface with a definite impact.

Mechanism divided the world into matter and energy; matter was composed of solid bits, energy of waves. Matter was primary for the waves of energy were fluctuations in a material substance. Now, suddenly, energy [like electricity and light] was composed of particles (Planck's quanta and Einstein's photons), and the atoms of matter were divided into particles having basically electrical properties. The fundamental distinction between electro-magnetic energy and solid matter was in danger of collapse and no one could shore it up.

Louis De Broglie took the next and most daring step. If light, which was thought of as a wave, now must be both a wave and a particle, should not matter, which was seen as particle, now also be seen as a wave? In 1927, a beam of Thomson's particles, now basic element of matter called electrons, was diffracted and produced interference patterns just like light. From then on, matter and energy were viewed as continuous, both exhibiting the dual properties of waves and particles.

Following up Thomson's work on particles, Ernest Rutherford, in collaboration with his student Niels Bohr, began to lay bare the structure of the atom. They built up a rough picture of the atom as a miniature solar system: The center was a heavy, charged nucleus surrounded by electrons in definite orbits. At first, these sub-atomic particles were thought of as little bits of matter; they became the basic billiard balls of the material world instead of Dalton's atoms and the classical ideal of materialism again appeared intact. But there were several problems. An electron may occupy a definite orbit, but when bombarded with energy from outside, it is knocked into a higher orbit; or, if the energy is sufficient, out of the atom altogether. But the orbit it enters is always discrete and precise so that either the electron leaps from one orbit to another without occupying any space in between, or else it moves gradually from one orbit to another but, in Rutherford's words, "knows beforehand where it is going to stop". Neither concept made much sense. The model of the atom as a miniature solar system with the electrons traveling in orbits was extremely imaginative and fruitful but the basic concept of an electron's orbit was mysterious and paradoxical.

De Broglie had suggested that electrons traveling through space have the same dual properties of waves and particles that were perplexing the students of radiation. Erwin Schroedinger extended De Broglie's conception to electrons within the atom. Schroedinger put the death blow to classical materialism with the suggestion that the electrons within the atom were not tiny billiard balls traveling planet-like in orbits but were waves propagating at discrete frequencies.

Under certain conditions, waves are not smooth and continuous but, rather, exist at only discrete frequencies. A piano string of a certain length and tension will only vibrate at certain frequencies; that is, will only give off certain tones. A column of air, as in a clarinet, likewise only vibrates at certain frequencies and plays certain discrete notes. On any of these frequencies, incoming energy is stored in the vibrations and produces sound. At other frequencies of vibration, the waves do not persist, no energy is stored, no sound produced. An electron could be a system of waves propagating at certain frequencies. At some frequencies it stores energy; these would be the energy level of the wave in Planck's term of a quantized wave or the so-called orbit of the particle. When energy is introduced into the atom, if it is of the right frequency, it will cause the matter-wave to change pitch, to rise to a higher register, to store more energy. Not really a particle deciding on a discrete orbit, the electron is, rather, a wave which can only vibrate or store energy at certain frequencies.

Heisenberg brought the Rutherford-Bohr image of the atom as composed of particles together with Planck's idea of quantized energy to form a new type of physics called quantum mechanics. Heisenberg took the standard wave equations and applied them to the sub-atomic matter waves and the formulas worked to account for sub-atomic behavior. Mathematically, it worked beautifully but the very success at the mathematical level led to tremendous problems at the conceptual level.

Being wave equations, the formulas of quantum mechanics seem to imply that the basic units of matter are waves. But waves of what? There is no way to answer that question, Heisenberg said, we should give up trying to picture what matter is made of, and concentrate on mathematical refinement. Wave equations are used because they work well to correlate experimental results, not because they describe the way the world really is. One can speak of electrons as simply waves, or as a matter-wave duality, or as wavicles, but we don't know what any of that means; we have no analogies from our ordinary experience to fit the sub-atomic level and so we can form no picture of it. The quantitative success of quantum mechanics comes at the price of failure at the qualitative level; the power of the equations is paid for by the weakness of the conceptions. Modern physics is strictly mathematical.

Immaterialism

The foundation of our ordinary world is occupied by inhabitants that appear very unlike the inhabitants of that ordinary world. Occupants of the ordinary world generally have such properties as solidity, mass, color, malleability, tensile strength, roughness or smoothness, softness or hardness, etc.. If one goes directly below the ordinary world to the molecular level, some of these properties already disappear. Molecules have mass, density, etc., but no individual molecule has a certain color, is soft or hard, malleable or not. These are properties of the aggregate of molecules we call the ordinary world, but the individual molecules themselves do not possess them. Looking at a single molecule, one cannot deduce or predict the color, softness, roughness of the aggregate.

Below the molecular level, atoms lack some of the characteristics of molecules. A molecule may have certain structures -- those that allow it to bond with others, chemical properties, acidity, etc. -- that atoms do not possess. One cannot tell from studying an atom of hydrogen whether it is a part of a molecule of water, hydrochloric acid, or whatever. Yet molecules of water and hydrochloric acid have different properties from each other and from the individual atoms that make them up.

Likewise, the "particles" which make up the atoms have even fewer of the properties that make up the ordinary world. Electrons have no color; neutrinos have no mass; neutrons have no electrical charge; waves have no density. One could not tell from looking at an electron whether it was part of a helium atom, a hydrogen atom, a piece of carbon, or what. Heisenberg has suggested that at even more microscopic levels, there may not even exist time and space as we know them.

The foundations of matter may be said to be material but it must be recognized that they are not material in the same sense as our ordinary world. Characteristics we associate with the ordinary world, those that were most important in defining the "material" that was the basis of classical materialism -- mass, density, texture, solidity -- do not exist at the micro-level. We must use what classical theologians called a _via negative_ (a way of negation) to describe the foundations of matter; matter is made up of waves, but not waves in any medium; matter is made up of particles but particles unlike any pieces of matter. Our conception of matter is formed on the basis of our ordinary experience but this world is just one small domain of nature and these conceptions apply only tangentially to the micro-world.

Complexity

The micro-world is incredibly complex. What began in the classical scheme as single atoms has become dozens of newly-discovered sub-atomic particles or wavicles. Where there were once only single atoms, Rutherford and Bohr substituted two or three particles. These have turned out to be only the longest lived version of many, many particles, some of which last only the tiniest fraction of the tiniest fraction of a second. Instead of two or three particles, there are now several classes of particles, each class often containing a multitude of particles.

Besides increasing numbers, theoretical considerations have led to the discovery of particles with no analogy to ordinary phenomena. As a corollary of Paul Dirac's equations governing sub-atomic interactions, there was no way to distinguish electrons which have a negative charge from a similar particle having a positive charge. Such particles would have no function in the atomic system; yet Dirac's formulas were so successful that they were accepted even with this bizarre result. Then in 1933, particles came to light that fit Dirac's description of a positively-charged electron, called a positron. When a positron and electron collide, they annihilate themselves in a burst of energy. Once the possibility of a positron, or anti-electron, was recognized, why not an anti-proton? If anti-protons combined with an anti-electron, you would have anti-hydrogen. If anti-hydrogen, why not a whole universe composed on anti-matter? In our world, such particles would be short-lived. They would collide with their double and destroy themselves. But that does not rule out the possibility of whole galaxies and universes -- perhaps the mirror image of our own, made up of anti-matter. Richard Feynman postulated that anti-matter is ordinary matter traveling backward in time. In expounding this, he developed a new theory of particle interaction for which he won the Nobel Prize.

Another theoretical problem involved the amount of energy exchanged in certain atomic reactions. As techniques of measurement and calculation became more precise, it was apparent that some equations did not balance and some energy was not accounted for. This led Wolfgang Pauli to posit the existence of a particle to carry off this energy; he called it a neutrino. Since all the major parts of the reaction are accounted for -- mass, charge, etc. -- the neutrino would lack all of these. At most, it might carry off its energy spin or angular momentum. Soon the idea of a particle with no mass and charge and few of the other things we take as constitutive of physical reality became part of the physicist's world.

The relative simplicity of the categories we use for the ordinary world do not equip us to understand the micro-world: Particles with no mass or charge, waves that propagate with no medium, a whole other world of anti-matter, a micro-world travelling backward in time. None of these are true of the matter we ordinarily experience and yet they appear true of the foundations of the world we see. Classical materialism has proven too simple.

Matter and Energy

Another characteristic of the micro-world is the interchanging of matter and energy. The distinction between them and the priority given to matter were keystones of the mechanistic picture. Again, Newtonian science took images that seemed true of the ordinary world and applied them throughout nature. At the ordinary level, much energy is transmitted through matter: sound, heat, force, all apply to matter vibrating, undergoing molecular motion or being struck. But the distinction between matter and energy and the priority of matter break down at the sub-atomic level. Einstein predicted that mass was the inertia of energy in the famous equation that $E = MC^2$. Thus, matter could turn into energy or energy into matter. Mass is "frozen" energy. The discovery of anti-matter revealed that when two particles of matter -- an electron and positron -- collide, they give off energy, usually in the form of gamma radiation. Two wavicles, modes of frozen energy, combine to form wavicles going off at the speed of light, usually as gamma radiation or gamma-ray photon (massless; i.e., with no "frozen energy"). Conversely, a gamma-ray or any form of electro-magnetic radiation can be considered as "particles" of matter. Each particle then has not only mass and charge but also an energy coefficient, correlated with the frequency of its wave which represents its potential to be translated into pure energy.

The immutability of matter, one of the foundation stones of classical science, vanishes. Not only can one produce atoms from other atoms by bombarding them with accelerated particles, one can transform some particles into others. Particles can be created from other particles or from sheer kinetic energy. One can no longer speak of the elements as fixed species of matter, nor of matter itself as fixed species. It is constantly undergoing transformations and fluctuations.

The more one penetrates into the depths of matter, the more energy is required. It takes some energy to tear a piece of paper; more energy is required to separate the atoms within the molecules that make up the paper. An incredibly greater amount of energy is needed to smash these atoms and to transform the particles that make up the atoms, the required energy is almost inconceivable. As one approaches the depths of matter, one approaches sheer energy. The atomic nucleus, as nuclear fission has shown, contains more energy than the molecules that make it up. You get more energy from smashing atoms than from burning the molecules of wood. The smaller particles that make up the nucleus contain much more energy. Particles even smaller than the nucleons (those making up the nucleus) contain incredibly more energy. One of the reasons the final depths of matter may never be plumbed is because of the almost infinite amount of energy required to work at these depths.

Immaterial Materialism

What is left of classical materialism? The ordinary world remains solid and material, but it rests upon a micro-world that cannot be called material in the same sense as the ordinary world. As we shall see, some claim that modern physics generates a kind of metaphysical idealism -- that the world is mind or spirit. Modern physics does not necessarily entail idealism in the traditional sense that the world is really insubstantial and mental (nor any other metaphysical doctrine). The ordinary world is as physical and substantial as it ever was. But ideas about matter are radically different now than in the days of Newton's billiard balls. The old materialism no longer applies to the foundations of matter. Shorn of solidity, immutability, density, texture, clear-cut boundaries (perhaps all boundaries in time and space) the foundations of matter resemble what classical science rejected as being immaterial or spiritual. If one wants to be a materialist and say that matter is the only thing that exists, one must mean by this something quite different, quite more paradoxical, more mysterious and open-textured than did classical materialism.

Spirit and Matter

Classical materialism brought tremendous conflict between religion and science by denying the presence of the divine spirit in the world (and the human spirit in man). Modern science, however, rather than denying the presence of the Spirit, provides a constructive image for understanding the relation of spirit and matter. Nature can be organized in a series of levels: the ordinary world, the molecular world, the atomic world, and quantum level (and perhaps levels hidden below the domain of quantum mechanics). Each is relatively independent of the others, for some characteristics exist at one that have no analogy at another, some laws apply at one and not at others, etc. Yet each depends upon the prior one and gives rise to the next. As one progresses down through these layers of nature, one gets further away from the material and substantial aspects of the ordinary world. The immaterial gives rise to the material, the insubstantial to the substantial. Immateriality is not antithetical to matter as classical science thought; rather, the immaterial is the source and ground of the material world.

It has been hard to specify what 'spirit' means (it is impossible if we are restricted to terms drawn from the ordinary, physical world). Traditionally, the term has meant what is not matter, what is immaterial. But what does immaterial mean? Obviously, the simplest definition is that the immaterial is what lacks the characteristics of matter. Thus, in classical theology, the divine Spirit was often described by a <u>via negativa</u>: God is not finite, God is not limited, etc.. It was easier to say what God was not than to say what he was. Likewise, the micro-world lacks the characteristics of the ordinary world, and so when modern science attempts to give a qualitative description of the sub-atomic world, it, too, resorts to a via negativa. Contemporary physics has the same problem of language as contemporary religion -- how to talk about something in words drawn from the world of tables and chairs which is not an inhabitant of the world of tables and chairs. Of course, physics has recourse to the meta-language of mathematics, but whenever it attempts to speak qualitatively, it runs into problems analogous to those of the theologian.

Modern physics, while not demonstrating the Spirit's presence in the physical world, undercuts mechanistic arguments against that possibility. Modern physics also offers helpful models for understanding the relationship of spirit and matter. The micro-world's not being material in the same sense as the ordinary world, the material world's grounding in an immaterial one, the impossibility of speaking directly about this ground of the natural order -- are all analogous to the claim of the church fathers that the physical world is the continual creation of the divine Spirit within it.

Indeterminacy

Newton's laws of motion implied that the future behavior of any body was determined for all time by the relevant positions and forces since his formulas apparently allowed one to calculate and predict the behavior of masses on the basis of the position and forces acting upon them. Increasingly, Newton's laws were verified in one domain after another, until it seemed only logical to conclude that they held universally. In the eighteenth century, Laplace carried this to its logical conclusion by claiming that the universe was a gigantic mechanism running according to Newton's laws. If one could know all the positions and velocities and other factors affecting the system, one could predict any occurrence. The behavior of everything in the universe was pre-determined for all time. Laplace postulated a super-being who could know all the relevant data, and therefore calculate the future. There were no elements in the system that were not pre-determined, no elements of chance or contingency.

Even on its own terms, Laplace's hypothesis was a gross extrapolation. In fact, Newton's laws only applied to a part of the universe. Newton was concerned with understanding certain domains of phenomena. Laplace applied this system of mechanics, not to particular domains, but to the entire cosmos. Also, Newton's laws were an abstract, mathematical idealization. Even in the particular domains under consideration, there could not be found the perfectly rigid bodies or perfectly straight lines and the inertial motion demanded by his formulas. They fit the real world somewhat loosely. Laplace's cosmic machine was a gigantic extrapolation from particular domains to the entire universe, and from the rather messy world to an ideal world where machines run without wearing out, and events fit perfectly the mathematical idealizations of Newton.

This extrapolation was not warranted by appeal to Newton's laws or any other scientific findings. Rather, it was a more philosophical claim growing out of the science of mechanism. Such a philosophy was not necessary to Newtonian science: One could perform the Newtonian calculus without conceiving of the universe as a machine. The success of the model of the _Principia_ in many areas led to the assertion that the cosmos ran like a machine. Although based on a great <u>generalization</u>, determinism was a <u>reductionistic</u> philosophy. The diversity of phenomena that would appear in the world can be reduced to the working of a few simple quantitative laws. It was not the quantitative aspect of Newtonian mechanics that gave rise to determinism -- one could calculate the rate of falling bodies or planetary velocity without seeing the universe deterministically -- rather, it was the extension of the drive for simplicity into a reductionistic approach that claimed that beneath the apparent complexity of the world were a few simple, mechanical laws.

As the apparent simplicity of materialism began to break down, so also with determinism. Planck and Einstein discovered that energy did not travel in continuous waves but in discrete quanta. Light sometimes appeared like a wave -- it could be diffracted, show interference patterns, etc. -- and sometimes like a particle. The same characteristics fit the newly discovered sub-atomic particles. If you passed a beam of them through a cloud-filled container called a cloud chamber, they left a trail like a series of small bullets. However, if you sent the same beam through a barrier with two holes in it and onto a photographic plate, you get a series of dark and light bands, just like a beam of light waves. Through one hole, the beam of electrons makes a single splash on film; with two holes you get a series of bands. If you think of the electron as a particle and ask which hole it went through, there is no way to tell. It is not behaving like a single particle but like a wave for the series of light and dark bands (called an interference pattern) is what you get from sending a wave at a barrier with two holes in it. Like light, the newly uncovered particles were found to behave like both waves and bullets. Waves spread out infinitely; particles are localized. If a particle acts like a wave, how can we know where it is? The fact is, we can't. In the experiment with the two holes, we couldn't determine where it was at any given point. Even if one conceives of an electron as a particle, it is a very paradoxical kind of particle -- one that shows interference patterns and whose position cannot be definitely established.

On the other hand, if it is conceived of as a wave, other problems occur. When De Broglie and Schroedinger quantified the idea of electrons as waves, they said the energy of the wavicle is inversely proportional to the wavelength. A single wave with a sharply-defined wavelength extends itself through space; in order to have waves concentrated in a single place, there must be a series of waves with wavelengths that cancel each other out and bunch up. A single wave has wide extension and cannot be localized; a large number of waves can be localized. The energy of a wavicle can be referred to as either its velocity as a particle or its frequency as a wave, but since energy is inversely proportional to wavelength, a well-defined velocity (energy) means small spread in wavelength, which means great extension in space. Therefore, if you know the velocity of an electron, it is only by conceiving of it as having a small range of wavelengths, which means it has great extension in space, and you don't know its position very well. If you know its position, that means it is localized, but localized waves mean many waves bunched together, and so you have many waves with a wide range of energies and velocities. Newtonian mechanics needed both position and velocity to operate its deterministic calculus but in quantum mechanics the position and velocity of an electron cannot both be known accurately at the same time.

Probability

The usefulness of the wave picture can be retained by regarding the behavior of electrons as probable but not determined. One can calculate the probability that an electron will pass through one hole or the other in the barrier but one can not predict with certainty what will occur. The calculation of the position, or even the existence, of a specific electron is only probable. Quantum mechanics has come to regard the quantitative meaning of the term electron as being the probability that such a particle will be in such a place.

Probability was also useful in other areas. In radioactive decay, one can predict the time it will take a sample of radioactive material to decay but one cannot predict when any single atom will decay. If one puts the sample before a Geiger counter, one will hear an erratic and random series of clicks and not a smooth and synchronized one. Although one can calculate the over-all time of decay, one can only calculate the probability that any single atom will decay, or single particle be given off, at any one time.

Probability also came up in connection with a phenomena known as Brownian motion. A botanist named Brown discovered in the nineteenth century that sub-microscopic particles suspended in water exhibited erratic and random movements. This was the result of being struck by moving molecules but this discovery revealed that motion at the molecular level was random and unpredictable. One cannot predict exactly the movements of the molecules, and therefore, the path of the particles in their way.

Probability is profoundly paradoxical: Although we can predict with stunning accuracy the behavior of the groups, we cannot predict anything about the behavior of the group's members. Brownian motion reveals that individual molecules move in an erratic and random way; yet the aggregate of gas molecules follows exactly Boyle's Law, so that we can accurately predict the temperature of a gas under pressure. We can predict how the aggregate of molecules behaves without being able to say much about the behavior of any individual molecule. The rate at which specific radioactive materials decay is quite precise -- it is called the half-life and is what enables a paleontologist to determine the age of a fossil. Yet we have no way of telling when a specific atom will decay or a specific particle be emitted. Events at the atomic level are random and erratic, yet they result in a totally predictable rate of decay. Or, insurance companies can predict that a certain percentage of men of a certain age will die of heart attacks. Who stops the heart attacks from happening when the quota from that age group has been used up? To say that many smaller influences "cancel out" each other does not help, for it doesn't explain how such random cancellations are always in the direction of the same precise result.

Observing

Supposing one, hypothetically, wanted to observe an electron. One must shine a beam of light onto it. Ordinary light has too wide a wavelength; one could not even find the electron for the width of the wavelength; but gamma-rays might do so. So one shines a beam of gamma-rays on the electron. The particle might have been at rest or in a certain orbit but being struck by the gamma-ray imparts energy to it, forcing it to move in a new way. In the beam reflected back, you observe not where the particle is now but where it was when first struck by the beam. The motion has been disturbed by an unknown amount, since the energy imparted to the electron is governed by Heisenberg's uncertainty principle. If you shine a flashlight on a house, the force of the photons striking it doesn't budge it; but in the realm of tiny, tiny particles anything striking them causes them to move. Thus, quantum mechanics reveals an apparently necessary degree of uncertainty in our knowledge of the world for the very process of studying that domain alters it.

Mechanism and Modern Science

Implicit in all that has been said, is the model of various levels. Each level within nature is relatively independent of, but also influenced by, the others. Characteristics occur at one level, but not at another; hardness, color, texture at the ordinary level; acidity, certain types of bonding, and motion at the molecular; at the sub-atomic, almost all the traits we assign to ordinary matter vanish. Yet each is dependent on the prior one: Particles make up the atom, atoms make up the molecules, molecules make up the substances of our ordinary world. Although there is a high degree of quantitative determinism at the ordinary level, beneath this the degree of indeterminancy or probability increases until at the quantum level (according to current theory) there is only probability. Just as what appears to be solid substance at one level is so much open space at another and the lack of anything solid at the most basic level, so what is deterministic at one level rests upon indeterminacy at another.

According to mechanism, influences worked from the lower levels to the higher and so the behavior of any system was explicable in terms of its parts. However, the state of the system is not only influenced from "below" (so to speak). Extreme heat or velocity at the level of chemical substance can produce changes right down to the atomic, and maybe even the sub-atomic, levels. Apparently this happens at the center of stars. The smaller parts do not simply create and determine what goes on at the upper levels, but rather, there is a series of semi-autonomous levels within nature with reciprocal relations among them. The ideal of reducing everything to a few, simple deterministic laws has been abandoned. Different laws and different entities appear at different levels, and the causal laws at the ordinary level are the product of contingencies and randomness at the microscopic level. Its reductionism and tendency to over-simplification mean that mechanism is no longer a viable option for understanding nature.

Conflict Diminished

Mechanism attempted to reduce all the phenomena in the universe to a few simple laws. Modern physics has shown this to be an impossible objective. The universe is too complex and multi-leveled to be reduced to a few simple laws and many of the laws that have been uncovered are not deterministic but contain elements of indeterminacy and contingency. Determinism, like materialism, brought conflict with religion. Now, however, claims to reduce all of nature or human life to a few, simple, deterministic principles must be looked on with skepticism. Research programs based on an ideal of scientific explanation as the reduction of phenomena to a deterministic calculus can be legitimately seen as outmoded. The religious believer need not reject deterministically-oriented results which are fashioned for limited domains: Gases do obey Boyle's law and planetary motions follow Newton's principles, and human behavior is often the result of environmental conditioning. But such mathematical formulas as Boyle's law or Newton's laws or the principles of operant conditioning do not exhaust the system of nature or the complexities of human life. That there are elements of mechanism, determinism, and conditioning need not be disputed; that they are all that there is, modern physics has rendered questionable, to say the least.

The break-up of the mechanistic empire and the rise of modern science with its more open-textured view should diminish conflict between religion and science and give both sides a tolerance for a variety of approaches to nature and human life. This is a purely negative result, certain impediments to religious claims in the modern world have been removed. It would be too strong, I think, to go beyond this negative result and claim that modern physics, <u>proves</u> the existence of human freedom or divine intervention. However, later we will see that modern science provides analogies (rather than proofs) to help the believer understand nature in relationship to God.

CHAPTER SIX:

THE DIFFUSION OF METAPHYSICS

More than a way of doing science, mechanism was a vision of reality. Part of its popularity, apart from the control of nature which it brought, was the neatness of its imagery. Easily grasped was the picture of the well-running watch, and the language of levers and pulleys. Thus the model of the machine became the lens through which everything was seen. The revolution in physics at the turn of this century shattered that lens. While still appropriate for some phenomena, mechanism is no longer the key to the entire spectrum of reality. With that lens broken, new ways of seeing have to be fashioned. Some insisted that the coming of the new science changed nothing metaphysically or religiously but as the more paradoxical and open textured imagery of the new physics diffused out from laboratories and conference rooms, others found in them the material with which to construct a new perception of the world to replace the gears and wheels of Maxwell's <u>Matter in Motion</u>.

Compartments Sealed

In the context of mechanism's challenge, the drive to compartmentalize religion and science, spirit and matter, arose. If such dualisms represent truth, then a change in context should not alter their claims; rather, mechanism's assault on religion should be praised for uncovering the proper relation between disciplines. While acknowledging that physics has drastically changed, Paul Tillich warned theologians in no uncertain terms "not to use scientific discoveries to confirm the truth of faith." "There is no justification... at all," he wrote bluntly for drawing on the categories of modern physics when discussing theological issues for "physical theories...have no direct relations" to religious issues. Making it clear that he felt that developments in science should have no impact on religion and that the theories of contemporary physics do not alter its fundamental relation to theology, Tillich summed up his argument by saying, "Theology, in using physical theories in this way confuses the dimension of science with the dimension of faith."

There is a sense, which we will get to

momentarily, in which this is obviously correct; but there is another sense in which it seems profoundly misguided. Taken in its strongest way, Tillich's argument implies that what happens in science can and should have no impact on what happens in theology, a procedure Tillich himself knows is false. His impulse to totally separate religion and science did not arise in a vacuum but rather came precisely in response to changes in science; i.e., the transition from Aristotelianism to mechanism. Tillich's life work -- the translation of traditional theological language into a more philosophically precise one -- is directly necessitated by developments in science. God must now be spoken of as the ground of being rather than a divine person beyond the sky, because science has shown such a medieval "three-story" cosmological image (God above, hell below, earth in the middle) to be absurd. In his discussion of miracles, Tillich just assumes the mechanistic regularity of the universe as understood in Newtonian physics, and so calls miracles "sign-events" and insists that "Miracles cannot be interpreted in terms of supernatural interference in natural processes." The point is not to criticize Tillich's artful redefinition of divinity and miracles but only to suggest that the need for such theological moves comes from the impact of natural science on religion. If it were true that religion and science live in separate vacuum chambers and that "physical theories....have no direct relation" to theology, then there would be no reason not to go on using the traditional imagery of a "God beyond" and of miraculous incursions into natural regularities and Tillich's agenda would be unnecessary. Thus, it seems clearly wrong to imply that the transition to modern physics could, or should, send no ripples through the theological world.

A much more carefully nuanced statement of the same position is wrought by John Dillenberger in the conclusion to his historical study, <u>Protestant Thought and Natural Science</u>. Having surveyed several centuries of inter-relationship between theology and science, Dillenberger is aware that two disciplines cannot be hermetically sealed from each other; but he is as anxious as Tillich to argue that there is no "warrant for basing philosophical and religious ideas on specific conceptions in the new science." He is particularly vehement against those who take the fall of materialism to automatically mean the re-ascendency of the spiritual: "In and of itself, the concept of energy or wave is neither more or less materialistic, nor more or less spiritual." Nor is it appropriate to resurrect the categories of freedom and God's action in light of Heisenberg for such a procedure equates God's agency and freedom with "disorder." Dillenberger's fundamental stance is that understanding matter as waves, or natural law as probability, are specifically <u>scientific</u> issues which should not concern the theologian. "The problem of causality is fundamentally a problem in science. It may or may not have metaphysical implications for other areas of thought," Dillenberger writes, and "the respect for mystery which has emerged in contemporary science does not necessarily imply a spiritual or religious interpretation of the world."

At best, Dillenberger suggests that some constructive "analogies" may emerge to relate religion and science. Even here, he is exceedingly circumspect and very critical of common ways of drawing parallels between the disciplines -- for example, seeing them as "complimentary" a'la Bohr's image of the wave-particle duality. While acknowledging the human longing for some unified vision of truth, he undercuts it with a Protestant-Kantian insistence on human finitude -- "human pretensions, and the sheer vastness and transitional nature of knowledge make it impossible for us to achieve such unity". To attempt a synthetic vision is not only to transgress disciplinary boundaries but also to fall prey to the sin of <u>hubris</u>. Admitting that his comments are "almost totally negative", Dillenberger is sure that "Those who separate the disciplines of theology and science...are basically more correct than those who too easily find relations between them."

Like Tillich, Dillenberger is obviously right when he says, "Scientific processes do not, in themselves, give theological meaning." But the question is, what does give meaning to theological words? If a philosopher or theologian uses such terms as matter, causality, nature, origin of the universe, time, etc., can they overlook the meaning of these terms in a scientific context, especially in a culture where science has become the major creator of meanings? It seems to me that the answer is clearly no. It is too strong for Dillenberger to say that, for example, the physical discussion of causality "may or may not have. . . implications for other areas of human thought." It would be very difficult to use the term causality, for example, without any reference to its meaning in either Newtonian or contemporary physics. When the eighteenth and nineteenth century thinkers, who Dillenberger discusses, used the term causality, say in their analysis of miracles, they obviously had in mind the Newtonian picture of mechanical causation. It is too much to ask that now the meaning of terms be kept completely distinct from one field to another when that has never been true historically. Since the age of reason, science has replaced religion as the creator of meaning, and if contemporary science has given new meanings to old terms or created new ones which theologians find fruitful, it is too methodologically puritanical to demand that these images not be used because they arose in science.

Both Tillich's blunt, and Dillenberger's careful, espousal of the compartmentalization of religion and science in the face of the new physics seem overly defensive and impossible to carry out. Unless the theologian is simply going to say nothing about such traditionally central religious concerns as the origin of the universe, the nature of life, and (in our case) the meaning of the physical world, he or she cannot help but take account of the new theories, outlook, and language generated by the revolution in physics. The place where both seem correct is in their insistence that the theologian must not base his or her theories on science or attempt to prove them by reference to science. The real animus in the argument of Tillich and Dillenberger is directed against the eighteenth century practice of natural theology, constructing demonstrations for religious beliefs on the basis of scientific theory. Thus, Tillich says, "The truth of faith cannot be confirmed by the latest physical or biological or psychological discoveries -- as it cannot be denied by them." To attempt to prove a religious conviction on the basis of science is to ignore the truth of Dillenberger's assertion that "Scientific processes do not in themselves give religious meaning." Scientists construct, validate, and use theories for their own purposes, and not to enter into theological disputes. Thus, for example, gaps in the causal nexus do not prove there is such a thing as freedom, no do gaps in the schema of evolution prove God's special creativity. All they prove is that there are gaps in the physical or biological theories which scientists may choose, for their own purposes, to leave blank (as Heisenberg did with his uncertainty principle), or to attempt to fill in with new scientific (not theological) concepts.

To found a theological system on science, as the seventeenth century virtuosi and Deists did is to court disaster. In this Tillich and Dillenberger are correct. Scientific terms and proofs arise from within science and get their primary meaning from that context. They cannot be equated with theological terms -- what the physicist means by wave or energy is not precisely what the theologian means by spirit or divinity. Science may change, may again become deterministic or something entirely different, and if theologians base their thoughts on science, they are in the sad position of always scrambling to keep up with new developments and then Barth is right -- the integrity of the theological enterprise has been compromised.

On the other hand, the climate has changed; the myth of the machine no longer dominates. Negatively, this means the defensive moves devised to respond to it are no longer necessary. Positively, it creates a climate of openness to a variety of models of the world which theologians can dwell in if they wish. It means there may be more possibilities to the use of analogy than Dillenberger's cautiousness allows for. The world is now seen by physicists in a new way; there is no reason why theologians should not look at it differently, too, if they wish. From the fathers of the church to the present, Christians have used the most rigorous system of language they can find in order to express their faith; there has never been a sanitized conceptual system marked "for theological use only". Justin and Origen are unimaginable apart from Plato and Albinus; Augustine could not have said what he did without Neoplatonism; where would Aquinas have been without Aristotle or Barth, for that matter, without Kant? Dillenberger wisely says that, "What happens in one area cannot become normative for the essential content of another," and the religious person using scientific terms must be conscious of their being used religiously and not scientifically. Since the eighteenth century, however, natural science has been the source of the most rigorous language we have (and it's been adopted by psychology, sociology, politics, as well as physics) and if the theologian adopts some terms and concepts from modern science, he is not contaminating his field with alien influences but is rather continuing a tradition that goes back to the fathers of the church.

After Physics

Struck by the revolutionary impact of the events in which they participated, many of the founders of the new physics turned from physics to metaphysics. Later in their lives, scientists like Werner Heisenberg, Erwin Schroedinger, James Jeans, and David Bohm focused their energy on the philosophical implications of the discoveries they had witnessed. While strident in his claim that quantum mechanics must give up speculating on the nature of the universe and stick with mathematical refinement, Heisenberg himself was never able to give up the temptation of philosophy. Towards the end of his life, he was particularly drawn to the Platonic image of the world as constructed out of geometrical forms. The transformation of particles into other particles, or into energy, showed matter and energy as one continuous reality. But throughout these transmutations, certain properties are never lost. These fundamental characteristics are always conserved and account for the orderly structure of sub-atomic reactions. Heisenberg and others called them "symmetries", and they represent, he argued, the primal forms of matter. From this, Heisenberg constructs a picture of matter very much like Plato's Timaeus. A universal, unformed matter or matter-energy continuum fashioned into an orderly universe by the imposition of certain mathematical patterns which are analogous to Plato's geometrical shapes. "If we wish to compare the results of present-day particle physics with any of the old philosophies," Heisenberg said in a talk given shortly before his death and published in Physics Today in 1976, "the philosophy of Plato appears to be the most adequate: The particles of modern physics are representations of symmetry groups and to that extent they resemble the symmetrical bodies of Plato's philosophy." Matter is basically mathematical, given its characteristics by the presence of geometric-like structures at its foundation. On one level, matter-energy is continuous but on another, it is differentiated into a series of patterns, or structures, which make the universe what it is.

While insisting that one could never penetrate experimentally to the depths of matter, Heisenberg, like Plato, believed that a mathematically-inspired form of meditation could reach the "central order of things." In his autobiographical essay Physics and

Beyond, Heisenberg reflects on a conversation with Wolfgang Pauli about the existence of a personal God. Heisenberg tentatively suggests that this central order of reality, reflected in the mathematical beauty of physics, might be analogous to a human "soul" and that "One can become aware of the central order with the same intensity as of the soul of another person." Heisenberg alludes to the mystical experience of Pascal -- the great seventeenth century French scientist and mathematician -- who was overwhelmed by an ecstatic vision of God and the universe which he kept completely to himself. This experientially appprehended soul, Heisenberg says, "refers to the central order, to the inner core of being whose outer manifestations may be highly diverse and pass our understanding." Tentatively then, Heisenberg finds in the quantum mechanics he was instrumental in developing an echo of Platonic science: A vision of the universe built from a few geometrical structures and possessing within itself a soul.

Erwin Schroedinger, too, ranged over a vast array of philosophical topics loosely connected with the theories of modern physics. One area that particularly concerned him was the role of mind, or consciousness, in the world of science. Natural science was developed, he argues in an essay entitled Mind and Matter, to study the world objectively and therefore to exclude the mind. Thus, we should not be surprised if we find no trace of the mind in science or in the world as seen through science, for science exists to systematically exclude it. The structure of science insures that the world will appear impersonal and dead. The irony, Schroedinger says, of objective science is that this very picture of the world which excludes the mind is itself the creation of the mind. The exclusion of the self from the process of knowledge is an act of the very consciousness which is excluded. The world seen through science arises out of the workings of our minds and yet, the mind remains alien to the world it has constructed.

Mind, then, transcends time and space because the categories of time and space and the view of the world constituted by them are creations of the mind. The world as uncovered by science is contained within the mind. Mind is not found in the world as pictured by science "because it is in itself that world picture." To Schroedinger, then, mind is primary to nature or science. This image of the knowing consciousness being prior to the physical world provides Schroedinger with a metaphor for reality. The cosmos is the product of a cosmic mind, just as the world of science is the product of the human mind. Science is, by definition, impersonal -- "No personal god can form part of a world model that has only become accessible at the cost of removing everything personal from it." But this means that science's concepts apply to only a small segment of reality. Before and beyond the physical world lies the universal mind and alongside of science exists the possibility of the reunion of the individual human consciousness with the cosmic mind which is its source.

A further extension of this argument can be found in the writings of Sir James Jeans. Quantum mechanics uncovers a world that cannot be pictured in any direct or literal sense. At best, we can fashion models or images of the world but these are not photographs or scale drawings but quasi-imaginary constructs. This shows, Jeans argues, that knowledge is a mental and not a physical, reality. Knowledge is a function of minds, not dead bits of matter. This is particularly illustrated by the famous experiment in quantum mechanics where an electron is passed through two barriers: If the barrier has one slit, the electron appears as a particle; if it has two slits or more, the electron behaves like a wave. Thus, Jeans argues, objectivity is an illusion. Rather than experimenter apart from his experiment, the very presence of the apparatus determines what is observed. Experimenter and experiment are a single system connected by the mind of the experimenter; the subject is no longer independent of the researcher. Quantum mechanics, then, Jeans argues, reveals the primacy of the subjective and the mental; notions of objectivity and materialism are built on top of a reality which is basically subjective and mental. "There is a certain presumption -- although certainly no proof," Jeans writes, "that reality and knowledge are similar in their natures, or, in other words, that reality is wholly mental."

The most far-reaching claim that quantum mechanics restructures our world is put forward by David Bohm, long controversial within physics for his repudiation of the accepted interpretation of the quantum mechanics called the "Copenhagen" school, which asserts that because it provides a full, mathematical account of the behavior of particles, the quantum theory is complete, even though it is only probabilistic and provides no qualitative models for the processes mathematically described. Bohm has consistently rejected this and urged researchers to probe behind the sub-atomic level of probable interactions to a prior level and uncover what are usually called "hidden variables", i.e., those sub-quantum forces that influence events at the quantum level. Beginning with a series of papers entitled, "Quantum theory as an indication of a new order in physics", Bohm has pushed beyond even traditional "hidden variable" theories to develop an entirely new view of the scientific enterprise which begins, with a perception of "unbroken wholeness".

Hidden variable theories imply that there must exist a "quantum interconnectedness" operating below the level of statistical interactions. This network of "causes" must be "non-local" -- that is, not bound by space and time. As described in his paper on an "Intuitive Understanding on Non-Locality", it is this aspect of hidden variable theories that drives Bohm beyond concern with particle interaction and to an insistence that this interconnectedness is its most fundamental feature.

Rather than start with the parts of the universe -- particles, waves, fields, interactions, etc., Bohm feels the "new order" of science must begin with a perception of "unbroken wholeness." In his later papers, Bohm wrestles with understanding this unbroken wholeness in terms of what he calls "implicate" or "enfolded" order. The picture which appears on the television screen is implicit in the broadcast waves, as music is implicit in the grooves on the record, or the magnetic arrangements on the recording tape. The waves or the recording mechanisms contain the picture and sound in an implicate way. Likewise, the unbroken wholeness of the universe implicitly contains the order that is the cosmos and this order is continually being unfolded or manifest in the phenomena of the physical world. Particles may appear as disconnected when they become manifest and localized, but they remain connected as part of the more fundamental unbroken order of the universe. Thus, Bohm envisions an entirely new kind of science that begins with wholes rather than parts. This new view of the scientific task and the universe it studies Bohm sees as implicit in the history of quantum mechanics and his radically new vision is but an unfolding of what lies hidden in the depths of quantum theory.

Many of the participants, then, in the scientific revolution at the turn of the century saw these developments as heralding more than just a new way of doing the same old task called physics. Rather, they saw them as ushering in a new vision of the physical world. In place of the materialism of the previous era, Schroedinger and Jeans argue for the primacy of a universal mind. In place of mechanism based on the interactions of distinct particles, Bohm develops a model of a fundamental strata of unbroken wholeness. Rather than a refusal to consider the spiritual within the context of the physical, Heisenberg echos Timaeus' cosmic soul at the heart of things; Schroedinger and Jeans defend the existence of a cosmic intelligence and Bohm points to an immaterial, unmanifest reality beyond space and time which is the ground of the manifest world. For all of these men, these are not "religious" concerns tacked onto their physics but images they find implicit in the transition from mechanistic to modern science.

New Light from the East

Probably the most striking result of the metaphysical diffusion following the collapse of mechanism is the rush towards rapprochement between western science and eastern mysticism. Ignoring the methodological structures of Tillich and Dillenberger (and of most modern philosophy of science) the claim that high-energy physics is uncovering the same truth discovered centuries ago in China and India is argued in three lavishly illustrated and compelling books: The Fabric of the Universe by Denis Postle, drawing mostly on the thought of Maharishi Yogi; The Dancing Wu Li Masters by Gary Zukav, using mostly Buddhist concepts; and the stunningly popular The Tao of Physics by Fritjof Capra, whose greatest affinity seems to be to Taoism and Hindhuism. All three books are intended as both introductions to modern high-energy and relativity physics for the non-physicist, and demonstrations of the convergence of physics and the eastern traditions; all three are written by western devotees of the east. Postle's book is based on a British television series which popularized the concepts of the new physics and he is content to intersperse quotations from the Maharishi or other Indian sources that sound similar to the ideas of physics. Zukav's work, too, is primarily a layman's explication of physics with a gentle undercurrent of suggestion that the physicist's experience of the world is that of the orthodox Hinayana Buddhist. It is Capra who argues most forthrightly that modern physics and eastern mysticism are "in perfect harmony".

All three seize upon the imagery of organic unity in modern physics. Whereas Newtonianism thought in terms of separate bodies, modern physics thinks in the imagery of fields, energy, interactions. Now nothing stands alone; all is a part of the one. The resonance with the Upanishads and the all-pervasive Brahma is obvious. Capra clearly sets forth this agenda when he writes:

> The basic oneness of the universe is not only the central characteristic of the mystical experience, but is also one of the most important revelations of modern physics... The unity of all things and events will be a recurring theme throughout our comparison of modern physics and eastern philosophy. As we study the various models of sub-atomic physics we shall see that they express again and again, in different ways, the same insight -- that the constituents of matter and the basic phenomena involving them are all interconnected, interrelated, and interdependent; that they cannot be understood as isolated entities, but only as integrated parts of the whole.

Capra points to the collapse of the distinction between the observer and the observed. In the experiment with the electron and the two barriers, the way the experiment was set up governed what was observed. There is no objectivity in the sense of an experimenter set apart from his material; rather, experimenter and experiment must be seen as part of a single process. Likewise, there is the unification of matter, space, and time in Einstein's general theory of relativity. As the apparent dualities of matter and energy, particles and waves are overcome in quantum mechanics, Capra says physics is pointing to the transcending and unifying of all opposites. The union of opposites, as contained in the Chinese image of <u>ying</u> and <u>yang</u>, is the fundamental structure of Capra's thought.

It is, however on theories involving elementary particles that Capra focuses his argument most eloquently. Central to eastern philosophy, as Capra understands it, is that "The world is conceived in terms of movement, flow, and change." As an analogue, Capra is drawn to field theories in quantum-electro dynamics, where particles are envisioned as the manifestation of fluctuating field. "The quantum field is seen as the underlying physical entity," Capra writes in a deft combination of physical and Upanishadic imagery, "a continuous medium which is present everywhere in space. Particles are merely local condensations of that field; concentrations of energy which come and go, thereby losing their individual character and dissolving into the underlying field." Matter, then, is a series of interactions. It is this continual series of movements -- captured on a bubble-chamber photograph with particles coming into existence, decaying into other particles, disappearing from the scene -- that catches Capra's eye as a physicist and a student of eastern thought. Theoretically, Capra's inclinations are towards Geoffrey Chew's "boot-strap" or "S-matrix" theory, which describes particles by a network of relationships, and attempts to understand the nature of particular particles by systemizing their patterns of interaction rather than, say, by breaking them down into even more fundamental particles. Of course, within physics, both field theory and boot-strap theory are controversial but both fit Capra's impulse towards conceiving of the fundamental structure of the universe by "laying stress upon movement, change, and transformation and regarding particles as transient stages in an ongoing cosmic process."

Zukav argues for the primal reality of an undifferentiated source in somewhat different terms. Rather than stressing the formalization of a network of relationships where a particle is conceived of as a special form of interaction, Zukav follows Bohm in trying to penetrate below all known patterns of interaction and find some "hidden variables" underneath. Behind the randomness of the sub-atomic world is an implicit order governed by connections beyond anything conceivable in ordinary terms -- such "superluminal" connections transcend time and space, and even Einstein's one invariance, the speed of light. They constitute a network of unbroken wholeness which represents the most fundamental structure of reality: the giveness of the universe. The cosmos simply "is" -- neither good nor bad, random nor orderly; it is simply what Zukav calls "that which is". Superluminal connections could point, Zukav argues, towards "superdeterminism" -- that everything must be exactly as it is, and nothing can be changed or altered. This view he finds similar to Buddhism in claiming that "no matter what we are doing at any given moment, it is the only thing that ever was possible for us to be doing at that moment." Whether such superdeterminism will pan out in physics is a very open question. Even without it, the basic trust of Zukav's argument remains -- that it is necessary to probe behind the quantum level for what Bohm calls "a new order" of unbroken wholeness", now that science sees the world as "a pure, undifferentiated reality".

While their expositions of contemporary theoretical physics are remarkable in their lucidity and elegance (clearly, they are among the best introductions available for the non-specialist), it is not as clear that modern physics necessarily points to the conclusion which Capra and Zukav draw. After the fall of mechanism, with its division of the world into autonomous bits of matter, the universe can obviously be conceptualized in a more unified way -- as a system of fields, an all-pervasive energy, or an inter-relationship of interactions; but it is not at all obvious tht this makes nature undifferentiated. Matter and energy are one continuous reality transformed into distinct forms under different conditions. But not just any forms. When one particle is bombarded with another particle, there are definite constraints on the set of resultant particles. Energy is put into a system and it comes out again as energy in different forms; but not just any forms. As Heisenberg always pointed out, several characteristics, called conservation laws, remain invariant throughout all interactions and determine what forms of energy will emerge at the end of the reactions. The basic task of physics is not only to conceptualize the underlying principle of unity but also to isolate the particular forms that are conserved in high-energy transformation in order to account for the fact that each reaction always produces some types of particles and never others. If the underlying form of the universe were completely undifferentiated, there is no logical reason why the interaction of any two forms of energy (particles) could not produce any conceivable other forms of the same energy but it is not so. These constraints, which produce diversity, are just as crucial to the structure of the universe as is the underlying field, system, or energy.

For example, the S-Matrix theory of interactions, which Capra favors, defines each particle, not as a separate entity but as a part of a system of interactions. However the very structure of the diagrams and the impulse behind producing them is not to blur distinctions between particles and interaction but rather to classify them into clearly distinct forms. The structure of the interactions themselves remain "unspecified" or "undifferentiated" but the preliminary and resultant stages of the interaction, the so-called "input" and "output" channels of the diagrams, which is to say, the particles going in and coming out of the interaction are far from unspecified or undifferentiated; they are, rather, governed by the structure of the diagram which is an analogue to the conservation principles.

From high-energy reactions, then, two aspects emerge as fundamental: energy or fields which might be termed the principle of unity and the conservation laws or constraints on the system which might be termed the principle of diversity. The problem with Capra's and Zukav's argument (but not with their expositions of physics itself) is that they over-emphasize the principle of unity and down-play the principle of diversity. Capra writes in a chapter ironically entitled, "patterns of changes" that "Both modern physics and ancient Chinese thought consider change and transformation the _primary_ aspect of nature, and see the structures and symmetries generated by the changes as secondary." I see no evidence from modern physics that the dynamic element must take precedence over the symmetrical element. The title to the chapter, "patterns of change" seems closer to the truth -- Physics focuses on change, but it is _patterned_ change that is important, and the correct understanding of these patterns -- call them symmetries, matrices, natural laws, conservation principles, or whatever -- is the core of physics for it is these patterns that account for the structure of the physical world. If the dynamic aspect were primary, there would be no patterns of change but only change itself without any comprehensible order. If that were true, any kind of physics would be impossible. To amalgamate high-energy physics and eastern thought, Capra and Zukav emphasize the element of universality to produce the impression that physics has decided that the cosmos is an undifferentiated unity as pictured in the Upanishades. Whereas, in fact, modern physics uncovers both principles of unity and principles of diversity.

111

This problem can be posed, and I think answered, in terms of another theoretical orientation -- general systems theory, developed by Von Bertalanffy, in an attempt to elucidate the general principles governing all living and interacting systems. One implication of general systems theory is that everything that exists can be seen as both a system in itself, and as a part of a larger system. When describing Plato's view of the universe as an organism, we saw that theories involving systems have this double-edged quality -- everything is simultaneously a part and a whole. Let us take an example from the field of psychiatry, and especially family psychiatry, where systems-theory has had particular impact. Persons with emotional problems can be understood and treated as individuals or as part of a system. Treated individually, the focus is on personal feelings, ideas, past history, etc. Treated as part of a system, the emphasis is on the function of their symptom within, say, the family. Here patterns of interaction become more important than individual thoughts, feelings, or behaviors -- perhaps the child's acting out brings his warring parents together, thus maintaining the family system; or perhaps, the husband's drinking allows the wife to feel superior because she must take care of him. Likewise, an electron can be isolated and its discrete properties (mass, charge, etc.) defined. It can also be seen in terms of its interactions in a particle experiment, or as a part of a hydrogen atom which is part of a molecule of water, which is a part of what I am drinking to assuage my thirst in order to live. Everything in the universe has this two-fold quality of being both a whole and a part.

Whether something is regarded as a whole or a part seems to be a philosophical equivalent of the quantum mechanical problem of measurement. In sending an electron through the barriers whether it came out a wave or a particle was a function of what apparatus was used; the observer and the observed were a part of a single system wherein the observer's intention altered the condition of the observed. In more trite and general terms, what we see is a function of what we are looking for. If I am pre-disposed to approach a man's drinking, or a woman's fears, in terms of past influences, then I will treat them individually, and take a detailed history, and probably not see that the man's drinking is his wife's one chance to take care of him, or the woman's fears keep her husband close at hand, and thus, their marriage together. Or, if I see them only as parts of a current system, I may not notice that even before he got married and started to drink, the man was overly dependent, first on his parents, then on his boss, and didn't start drinking until his wife went out and got a job, or that the woman was tyrannized by her parents and has always been shy and fearful. Whether I conceptualize the patient's problem in terms of family interaction or individual dynamics depends a lot on what orientation I bring to them, as well as on what my goals are in working with them. Likewise, whether I see diversity or unity as primary in the physical world depends on what tasks I am undertaking and what my basic orientation is. As I understand it, high-energy physics is in agreement with this implication of general systems theory that everything can be seen as a whole in itself, and as part of a larger whole. Whether one stresses parts or wholes, diversity or unity, discrete particles or general fields, depends on the task one is doing and the framework one brings. Thus, I suspect Capra and Zukav are led to a one-sided emphasis on unity and wholeness because of their theology and not their physics. Beyond this general principle of parts and wholes, both high-energy physics and general systems theory are seeking a model that transcends the distinction between parts and wholes. Such a theory would neither collapse the parts into the whole (as I suspect Capra and Zukav of following the Upanidshads in doing) nor see the whole as an epiphenomena of the parts as mechanism did. Rather, high-energy physics and systems theory are attempts to image a <u>unity-in-diversity</u>.

Philosophically, this is a problem which has never been finally resolved in the history of human thought. Tillich called it one of the fundamental polarities of being -- individualization and participation. Stereotypically, many of the conflicts in our world are regarded as conflicts over these polar opposites -- in economics between capitalism and communism; in religion between the western and eastern traditions; in politics between anarchy and totalitarianism, etc, and etc. Human thought seems to stagger from a one-sided emphasis on individuals and particulars to an equally one-sided emphasis on universals and collectivities. The fountainhead of eastern philosophy -- the Upanishads -- drives towards the totalitarianism of the universal -- all drops of water are to be dissolved in the vast ocean of being.

Modern Christianity (particularly the Protestant evangelical variety) forged its basic concepts in the eighteenth and nineteenth centuries when the impulse towards seeing the universe individualistically predominated. The thrust of much current Christianity is towards a spiritual atomism. My own bias, which I find reflected in modern physics (as well as general system theory) is not to react to the extreme individualism of modern Christianity by reverting to the equally extreme essentialism of the Upanishads but to find new images, such as unity-in-diversity, that transcend and maintain the integrity of both. Here I find Capra's and Zukav's relentless emphasis on the universal both a religious and scientific distortion.

The basic thesis of Capra and Zukav -- that modern physics sees matter not in terms of "isolated entities but only as integrated parts of the whole" rings true. But their implication that this is true of eastern thought in a way not true of western theology is false. Capra virtually equates the term "mysticism" with eastern religion as though there was no mysticism in the west. Certainly a physicist is not to be blamed for losing his way among the religions of the world (I have certainly lost my way among many a Feynman diagram) but, in fact, there is little in his description of the nature of matter that Justin, Irenaeus, Origen, Dionysious, Bonaventura, the medieval alchemists, or Jonathan Edwards would not find congruent with their own outlook. Also there is a question about what "integrated parts of the whole" means. It need not, and I think does not, imply an "undifferentiated unity" but rather, points to a unity-in-diversity which embraces both symmetries and fields, energy and its conservation principles, particulars and universals, and which is, therefore, closer to western vision of the universe. With that, we are already into our final chapter.

CHAPTER SEVEN:

THE BODY OF THE UNIVERSE

Towards a Theology of Nature

Running from the faith's founding fathers through the alchemists and perhaps including Newton, is a tradition whose major ingredient is a spiritual understanding of matter. For both theological and scientific reasons, it has all but died. Theologically, the post-Nicene fathers, to solve their own dilemma about three divine beings existing as one God, developed a doctrine of God as Trinity: stressing transcendence, rendering a consistent theory of divine immanence problematic, and making the relation between spirit and matter confusing, as the later Christological controversies revealed. The mainstream theological tradition has continued to define Deity as transcendence. Various events -- the dominance of mechanism, Kant's philosophy of finitude, the tramatic events of the two world wars, accelerated this trend in the modern period; most modern theological energy has gone into separating God from the world. Scientifically, as the image of the machine came to preeminence, divinity was left with no conceptual space and religion, along with God, was pushed further and further beyond the limits of reality. The main line of theological defense, often paralleling the separation of God and the world, was compartmentalizing religion and science. The result of this defensiveness was either stony silence or perpetual conflict until now, the student of theology assumes that religion and science have nothing to say to each other (except perhaps in the realm of ethics) and that the traditional task of forging a theological vision of matter is madness or heresy.

The coming of modern physics sweeps all that away, dethroning the twin absolutes of materialism and mechanism. The make-up of matter, the contents of the universe, the structure of scientific law -- have all been found more complex and paradoxical than eighteenth and nineteenth century researchers could have guessed. The mechanistic empire has broken up from within; new theories contain a much more subtle, flexible, and open-textured vision of nature. The polemics between religion and science, forged in the era of mechanism, can cease. This point, though important, is purely negative. Now, not only can conflict cease but a task more positive and constructive (but also more speculative and dangerous) can take its place. A new rapprochement between Christianity and natural science may begin: The earliest theological tradition of a spirituality of nature may again find expression.

A theology of nature must be distinguished from natural theology. Eighteenth century natural theology attempted to <u>prove</u> the reality of divinity by assuming that science describes the way the world is in some absolute way and that from that description, God's existence can be demonstrated. Along with a more open-textured view of nature has come a more open-textured view of scientific language. I do not think that science describes the world in an absolute or complete way, or that coercive proof for the existence of God is possible. Conceptual clarification, not proof, is the goal of this chapter: drawing analogies between the <u>language</u> of the scientist and the believer, pointing to certain continuities between the way each of them is speaking, raising the possibility of a vision that embraces them both.

A theology of nature is intended for the person seeking to understand the physical world in light of his or her experience of God. While drawing heavily upon natural science, no claim is made that current physical theories prove such a vision true. Rather the intention is to assist religious people in coming to terms with the physical world in a way that edifies and enriches their faith.

Such a theology of nature, as envisioned here, represents a stark repudiation of the major thrust of modern Christian thought. To the conservative, it will feel slightly heretical even though it recapitulates in modern language the themes of the church's first theologians. For Kant, Ritschl, and Schleiermacher, such a theology is logically impossible. To Barth, such an endeavor compromises the integrity of the theological enterprise. A defensive compartmentalization of religion and science, the dualism of matter and spirit, the displacement of mysticism by the ethics of obedience -- all these once-central themes are here undermined or reduced to minor status. Symbolically, such a theology represents a "return to Greece" (to use an image fashioned by James Hillman in another context). Such a return to the fathers is a two-edged sword. On one hand, it signals deep respect for tradition and continuity and a desire to build upon the foundations of orthodoxy. On the other, it indicates a longing for openness and the spiritual polymorphousness of those who so unselfconsciously drew on the best wisdom and science of their day to give expression to the faith that was in them. They knew no other way to follow the Lord's injunction to be like leaven that enriches the loaf of the world and Paul's admonition to bring all things under the dominion of Christ.

The Immanence and Transcendence Trap

The relation of God and nature has traditionally been discussed and confused by use of the terms transcendence and immanence. Some have sought to combine them; others to concentrate on only one. Aristotle's God was wholly beyond, the Stoics' logos wholly within. The influential schema of middle Platonism solved the problem with two gods; but Christianity claimed to worship only one and so could not take that path. Instead, the church opted decisively for transcendence after Nicene Creed, paying lip-service at best to the image of immanence. In response to the mechanistic model of nature as a closed and deterministic system, either transcendence or immancence was emphasized. Deism, folllowed by Kant, placed God outside the world; there was no room for him in the closed universe. The liberalism which followed Schleiermacher took the opposite position and placed the divine wholly within the natural order: God was seen as working through the mechanical processes of physics to such an extent that God became virtually identified with the forces of nature. Immanence-language emphasizes God's intimate ties to the world and his presence within it. Without such language, God becomes distant and irrelevant. Transcendence-language emphasizes God's freedom and independence of the world: Without such language, God becomes simply a more pious name for the forces of nature and another finite entity shorn of any sovereignty; being wholly within the natural order, he cannot overrule it and do anything "unnatural".

Modern discussions of divine transcendence and immanence began in the period of Newtonian science, whose language was conditional by the geometry of

Euclid: thus it was tacitly assumed that transcendence and immanence were <u>spatial</u> terms referring to three-dimensional space. God's transcendence meant distance in three-dimensional space so that God was "beyond the heavens" in the way that Jupiter is beyond Mars in the solar system. Likewise, God's immanence meant God was within nature, like gas under pressure is within a container. In the modern world, we need no longer define our terms spatially in this way since we are no longer bound to regard space as Euclidian and three-dimensional. New models for God's relationship to the world might be fashioned along newer mathematical models of multi-dimensional spatial relations. My concern, however, is with language and not mathematics. Such words are concepts, theories in miniature, that refer to the way in which we choose to <u>speak</u> about God and the world and not how we visualize God as an entity in Euclidian space. "Transcendence" and "immanence" set the limits in which our speaking takes place, rather than describe spatial relations. They are the ends of a spectrum along which thought moves; they are boundaries which our minds should not cross if they seek to be in continuity with what has been said before. "Transcendence" sets the boundary of the language of immanence; God cannot be so bound up with nature that he becomes identified with it, and inseparable from it, and so loses his independence. Likewise, "immanence" sets the boundary of the language of transcendence; God cannot be so transcendent that he loses contact with the world and cannot be conceived as present to it. In speaking about God's relation to the world, both his freedom and presence are to be maintained and not played off against the other. Within these boundaries the reality of the Spirit in the physical world will be explored, for the name usually given to the divine immanence or presence in creation is Spirit.

Spirit and Matter

The basis of matter is no longer visualized in terms of billiard balls but in images remarkably like those used to describe "Spirit" -- it lacks the qualities attributed to the stuff of the ordinary world; it gives rise to the solidity, density and extension of the ordinary world, without itself having much solidity, density, or extension; it must be described, therefore, by a <u>via</u> <u>negativa</u>. At its most radical extreme, the use of the via negativa implies that the ground matter is a nameless abyss which cannot be spoken of or comprehended at all -- an image from physics strikingly similar to the language of Plotinus, Origen, Dionysious, and Eckhardt. What science discovers as the ground of matter may not be what believers call God, but they speak about them in similar ways: The language of the immaterial as the foundation of the material emerges out of both science and religion, opening the possibility of a common vision.

Speaking of the immaterial as the foundation of the material makes us aware of the limits of our ordinary senses. The way in which this is true in science is easier to illustrate. We have probably all had the experience of looking at a cloud from the air or the ground and having it appear so solid that we felt we could walk across it. It appears solid because our eyes are sensitive to light photons which penetrate some things, like glass, and are reflected by most others. Light reflected off the clouds makes them look solid. Suppose our eyes were sensitive to x-rays photons instead; then everything would look like a fluoroscope picture -- many things that now "look" solid would appear as vacuous and insubstantial. Supposing instead that our eyes were sensitive to ultra-high energy particles (and that such particles could be focused); virtually nothing would appear solid and the whole concept of solid matter would be inconceivable. Fortunately, our eyes are sensitive to particles that are generally deflected by what our other senses regard as solid, so that we see walls (which we would not if our eyes were sensitive to gamma-ray photons) that we cannot walk through. Sometimes, they fool us, as when they give clouds the appearance of solid ground or when they fail to detect a plate glass window and we fall through the cloud, thinking it is solid, or bump into the window, thinking it is vacuous. Thus, our notion that ordinary matter is solid is, in part, relative to the fact that our eyes are only sensitive to light photons. To other kinds of eyes, "solid" matter would appear positively immaterial and ethereal.

Believers who speak of the presence of the Spirit in creation often use the language of perception. They speak of seeing, tasting, sensing the divine -- not, presumably, because their eyes have mysteriously become sensitive to high-energy photons but because, like the researcher in high-energy domains, they have become aware of the limits of their ordinary sense of the ordinary world. Because of the limits of our senses, we cannot see the physical world as insubstantial, although it would appear so from another perspective; likewise, we do not always see it grounded in the divine Spirit, but it appears so from another perspective.

The language of science is inherently impersonal while, especially in the west, religion has embraced more personalistic imagery when speaking of God. A wholesale adoption of images like energy and fields could result in a depersonalizing of religious language, a consequence more in line with the eastern philosophies favored by Capra and Zukav. One must keep in mind, however, Schroedinger's point that science frames reality in an impersonal way for its own purposes but these impersonal metaphors tell us more about the structure of our scientific disciplines than about the nature of reality. Religion does not, and probably should not, operate within the same set of theoretical constraints as natural science and so is free to envision the metaphores of immateriality generated by modern science in more personalistic ways. Schroedinger in his essay Mind and Matter, Heisenberg in Physics and Beyond and James Jeans in his philosophical writings have already indicated different ways of seeing in and through the language of modern physics personal as well as impersonal dimensions. Also, the fathers of the church traveled a similar path. The Stoic term logos was fundamentally impersonal but by taking it over and applying it to Jesus a two-fold intellectual movement transpired: Jesus was universalized through reference to this most universal category and the logos was personified through reference to this profoundly personal figure. The same sort of movement could take place in relation to the supposedly impersonal imagery of modern physics which, ironically, claims to describe the origin of the personal. Modern physics, then, recovers the ancient vision of an immaterial realm as the immanent source of the material world -- a vision which can be expressed in both the impersonal language of science and the personal language of devotion.

Freedom

Modern science reveals an inherent complexity too great to be reduced to a few simple laws, points out the limits inherent in scientific claims, demonstrates a system of relatively independent levels within nature, and uncovers a domain of probability at the heart of the matter. A further consequence of the current state of quantum mechanics is the loss of any qualitative description of the sub-atomic world. Since we cannot say exactly where an electron is or when a particle will be emitted, precise description eludes us. Accepting this, Heisenberg said that physics should turn from qualitative descriptions of the world to mathematical manipulation. Quantum mechanics brings physics qualitatively to a halt by concentrating only on quantitative refinement. Quantitatively we can describe relations of probability but we have no qualitative language for them. The domain of quantum mechanics can only be expressed by mathematics; no linguistic models are possible. When the natural order was seen as deterministic, it could be explained by mechanical analogies of watches and billiard balls. No such analogies emerge from quantum mechanics.

Philosophically the focus has shifted from describing the world to revealing the limits of science. Since we can know nothing beyond probability at the quantum level, we can give no precise description of the foundations of the physical world. David Bohm, the physicist-turned-philosopher-of-science, refuses to accept this. He is troubled by the fact that no explanation of why an electron moves where it does, or a given atom decays when it does, is possible. Bohm calls this apparent arbitrariness in nature the loss of causality. By causality, I do not think Bohm means determinism, a point his critics have consistently overlooked but, rather, inter-relatedness. When Bohm says we must re-establish causality in the sub-atomic sphere in order to describe why the electron moves and the atom decays as they do, he is trying to establish the inter-relatedness of events.

Can there be a description of the world that is not deterministic? Heisenberg implies that there cannot; to negate determinism, one must give up picturing the world. For most of Bohm's critics, too, his attempt to return physics to descriptions at the micro-level is a return to determinism. Bohm wants to give a description of the inter-relatedness of the universe (which is what he means by causality) without falling into determinism. For Bohm, to explain or describe something is to see its relations with other parts of the universe. A purely random and arbitrary event would bear no relationship to anything else in the universe. This system of relatedness is what Bohm calls causality; it need not imply mechanism or determinism; only inter-relatedness.

Bohm wants to emphasize the world's variety and complexity (he says that nature is "infinitely" complex) without giving up description and explanation altogether. The universe, with its variety of levels, entities, different types of laws -- is simply too complex to be reduced to a few deterministic and quantitative rules. Each level of matter is semi-autonomous and semi-conditioned by the prior ones. Under new conditions (new temperatures, velocities, energies, etc.), new kinds of relations may emerge. Given the complexity of the universe, any law or relationship is relative to certain variables, domains, and levels of nature, and none apply absolutely. Neither determinacy or indeterminacy are fundamental, Bohm says, but rather, the "infinite complexity of nature." Nature is too complex to be reduced to any single set of formulas, however, it is not too complex to be understood by a variety of categories and a sensitivity to the diversity of relations within nature. Inter-connections exist between phenomena but not all inter-connections are the same, not all are deterministic.

What is the religious person's stake in all this? Mechanistic determinism left no place for the divine initiative and freedom. God could either be immanent within the system but bound by it (as in the thought of Spinoza), or outside of it and irrelevant to it (as in Deism). God could not be both immanent and free. Mechanistic determinism also answered the formerly theological question of what held the universe together and made it whole. The universe was bound together by casual links and they formed one, whole, mechanically functioning unit. Given the breakdown of such casual connections and the collapse of the mechanical model, what conceptually holds the universe together? We could continue to insist on Newton's causal chains but they are too tight and have snapped. We could agree with Heisenberg and the current interpretation of quantum mechanics and say that such a question is meaningless and that quantitative refinement is all that is needed. We could follow Bohm and try for a new form of inter-relatedness that will take account of the fact that these inter-relations are more complex, open-textured, and "looser" than Newton and the classical investigators thought.

So far, little has been said about freedom, especially human freedom. It is exceedingly difficult to define what we mean by freedom. Freedom is a term in our ordinary language; it is not a technical term in some precise and scientific vocabulary and I am not sure we can get behind ordinary language to any more rigorous concept. What do we mean when we say that someone acts freely? We do not mean that his actions are random, chaotic, or unformed. A person who acted without any pattern would not be called free but insane. If a person acts in a fairly standard way, in accordance with what we call his character or personality, we still say he is free. We say a person is free even if we find some antecedent influences impinging on his action. We say a person is free even if we find some connection between his past actions and present ones. We say he is not free if we find connections and influences that coerce and bind him to act in a certain way. We say a person is not free if we cannot possibly imagine the act to have been different; we then say he had no choice. Generally, we say an act is free if we can, at least hypothetically, imagine that it could have been otherwise; then we say the person chose it.

In ordinary language, freedom functions to describe loose connections between events. Freedom does not imply that there is no background, history, form, connection, or relationship between occurrences but just that these do not determine the outcome in some coercive way. Supposing a student is choosing to go to college, or what kind of college to go to. Perhaps he agonizes over the decision, weighs several competing factors, asks several peoples' advice, and finally decides to go to one college and not another. Afterwards, one can see connections between his choice of colleges and his background, his temperament, the people whose advice he sought, etc. Yet, the presence of these connections doesn't lead us to say the choice was not free for such connections are loose, not deterministic, and we could hypothetically imagine him making the opposite choice for different reasons.

The term freedom, then, functions to describe a loose inter-connection between events. This is exactly the language we are looking for to describe the connection between certain phenomena. What would it mean to say that events in the world are free? It would not mean there was no connection between them. It would not mean that no pattern could be discerned. It would not mean that natural events have no history, no continuity between past and present. It would not mean there were no influences on events. It would mean that there are inter-connections between events, that there is an order to the universe, that patterns can be traced, just as it does when one says that human actions are free. It also means this order and regularity is not hard and fixed, not one-to-one, but complex, open-textured, and "loose" when compared with the mechanical ideal.

This is little help to the scientist but the scientist need not describe the regularities of nature in any but quantitative terms. Still, the complexity of nature, with its variety of entities and multitude of levels demands what Bohm called a "more general concept of natural law." Such a general description would discern connections between phenomena but connections of a more complex and open variety. Pointing to the freedom of the cosmos accurately underscores this open-textured nature of current scientific thinking.

This could, however, help the religious believer. Freedom is connected with actions and agents. The fact that we can legitimately describe the events of the universe as free does not prove there must be an agent behind them but it does make intelligible the believer's claim of divine initiative. The point is conceptual clarity and analogies of language, not proof from one field to another. The universe being the product of a free divine agent would suggest that events in the universe would have a pattern and an order but that these connections would not be rigid and coercive and that we could imagine the universe being other than it is which parallels science's description of the natural order. This does not prove, within science, that the religious claim is correct but it does suggest the possibility of a common language between them. The concept of real but open-textured connections between events emerges from both religion and science but each uses this common language for its own purposes. Divine transcendence is not a claim about three-dimensional space but a description of divine freedom and we can describe that freedom by pointing to the real but open, connections between physical events.

One example may illustrate this: Jacques Monod, in his powerful mechanistic account of the origin of life entitled <u>Chance</u> <u>and</u> <u>Necessity</u>, argues that life arose by chance. What does he mean by chance? Apparently, he means contingency; that life and the world it inhabits are not necessary and might have been other than they are. He obviously does not mean that there were no antecedent factors in the origin of life for much of his exposition is taken up with describing them -- the formation of certain chemicals, the atmospheric and climatic conditions, cosmic radiation, and so on. Rather, he means that none of these influences by themselves, or all of them together, dictated that life must come into being. The order in the world and the structures of life are not necessary; they could not have been predicted from the prior stage. Yet, once it happened, like the student choosing his college, connections can be discerned. The emergence of life was possible but not necessary; and the odds against it, given its complexity, were immense. By chance, then, Monod does not mean the absence of any connections but rather that such connections and events are contingent.

These characteristics of contingency are also the characteristics of free choice: What someone chooses to do freely is not necessary, or rigidly predictable; but it is a possibility with some connections with other possibilities. Contingency, the emergence of one possibility from among many possibilities, has the same characteristics as acts of volition, whereby one selects one possible choice from among many potentials. What Monod takes as signs of randomness can be taken as indications of willful choice. To say that life is contingent is compatible with life having arisen by divine choice.

By emphasizing the role of chance, Monod has built a more complex and ambiguous kind of natural law into the biological realm just as quantum mechanics, by emphasizing chance, has built a more complex and open view of natural law into the physical realm. In both realms, the elements of contingency and flexibility can be seen as the products of chance or of choice. Monod admits he is awestruck by the fact that chance alone could have produced such complex and varied creatures as bacteria and biologists, just as many physicists have been awestruck by the claim that chance gives rise to complexity and order of matter. Although confident that chance totally accounts for the origin of life, Monod says that even when "the miracle stands 'explained' it does not strike us as any less miraculous". Religion and science are two disciplinary accounts of a common mystery -- the awe-inspiring emergence of matter, order, and life from the midst of radical contengency: one in the language of freedom, the other in the language of chance.

Unity

Since the age of reason, science has defined itself as a method of <u>analysis</u>. Analysis, from the Greek word to loosen up, has meant loosening up the parts of something and breaking it down into its constituent pieces. To understand a chemical compound meant breaking it down into molecules. To understand molecules meant breaking them down into atoms. To understand atoms meant breaking them down into smaller particles. And now, in high-energy physics, to understand sub-atomic particles means seeing if they can be broken down into smaller ones -- currently called quarks. No doubt, when quarks are found, the attempt will be made to break them down into constituent structures. However, currently in high-energy physics, one of the most revolutionary developments (if not <u>the</u> most revolutionary) in the history of natural science is taking place -- the concept of analysis is itself breaking down. When molecules were broken into atoms, it seemed right to say that the molecule was made up of the atoms. When atoms were broken into sub-atomic particles, it seemed right to say that the atom was made up of particles. Now, if one particle is bombarded with another, many particles are produced; but they cannot be said to be the parts of the original particles in the same way in which, if an atom is smashed, the particles can be said to be parts of the atom. If a hadron is bombarded with a gamma-ray photon, one gets a shower of hadrons. But it makes no sense to say that the hadron is made up of hadrons. If one fires a positron at an electron, one gets another batch of hadrons. Yet the electron and positron are taken to be indivisible and it is not said that the electron is made up of hadrons the way in which an atomic nucleus is made up of neutrons and protons. Even more astonishing, some of the hadrons given off transform themselves into gamma-ray photons which, in an electric field, change into an electron and a positron. It makes no sense to say one has divided the electron into parts, one of which becomes itself an electron and anti-electron. A neutron bombarded with a pion gives a proton but no one now claims that neutrons are made up of protons. And so it goes. In the sub-atomic domain, one is not in fact breaking things up into their constituent parts, one is simply transforming something from one form to another. One can describe these transformations in terms of quarks with various characteristics (color, spin, flavor) of their own but the most basic fact is that in the sub-atomic domain, one has ceased to analyze in the old sense. One has ceased to break things down. One puts energy into a system, by bombarding it with a particle, and one gets energy out in another form.

One might expect this from Einstein's equivalence of matter and energy. Nothing was more revolutionary and destructive of the mechanistic synthesis than the short formula $E = MC^2$. Newtonian physics rigidly divided the world into matter and energy and gave priority to matter. Einstein claimed that these were different forms of one reality. Matter could be transformed into energy and from energy matter could be produced. This potentially undercut the drive to break matter down into smaller and smaller bits, for eventually, what one would get would not be smaller bits but sheer energy.

Instead of analysis, in the old sense, at high energies one is getting transformations of energy, or what could be called matter-energy. Matter and energy are one continuous reality which is transformed into different forms under different conditions but, as Heisenberg argues, not any forms. When one particle is bombarded by another, there are constraints on the set of resultant particles. Energy into a system comes out in different forms but not just any forms. Several characteristics of matter-energy are conserved in these high-energy reactions which determine what forms will emerge.

From the bombardment of particle with particle at high energy, two elements emerge: energy or matter-energy which is transformed into various forms plus certain constants, or "symmetries" which, by being conserved throughout the reaction, govern the various forms that the energy takes. The conservation of these symmetries accounts for the structure of matter and the universe. The question of why the universe or matter has certain forms and structures can be rephrased as the question of why these symmetries, which give it the form that energy assumes, exist.

Perhaps it has to do with the structures of space and time. The high energy transformations take place in space and time. The pion moves through space and time and strikes the electron and the hadrons are given off and spread through space and time and as time goes on, some transform into gamma-ray photons which decay back into electrons and positrons. Perhaps these symmetries are what allow energy to pass through space and time. Thus, matter is energy passing through space and time; or space and time impose certain structures on energy that give matter the form that it has.

Energy, matter, space, and time are then inseparable from each other; each must be defined in relation to the others: Matter can be seen as energy moving through time and space according to these symmetries; energy is known by its form, which is a function of its locus in space and time; space has the form that it has because of the presence of matter (according to Einstein's general relativity) and time, too, can be a function of energy, i.e., the velocity or gravitational locus of the timekeeper. Matter and time are, at some level, equivalent, for matter is given form by the necessity of matter-energy moving through time. The same conservation laws that govern the form of matter apply throughout time; it doesn't matter how fast time goes, or even if one goes backward in time; the same conservation laws apply (if a particle reverses in time, it apparently becomes its anti-particle, but the conservation laws and symmetries that make it what it is abide).

Thus, matter must be seen from two perspectives -- the perspective of energy that assumes the various forms we call matter and the perspective of the symmetries (perhaps necessitated by space and time) that control the form matter-energy assumes. Energy represents continuity, since matter-energy is continuous throughout. Focusing on energy and on continuity, however, is not enough. There must also be the perspective of the symmetries and of discontinuity, for matter-energy assumes distinct forms and regularities, which give the universe the structure that it has and make science possible. The symmetries and space-time, are the elements of diversity and plurality. Things are different and distinct because they exist in space and time, even though they arise from a common source in matter-energy. Thus, matter is the meeting place of both unity and diversity.

Even if these speculations turn out to be misdirected, these remarks illustrate two points implied by contemporary physics. <u>First</u>, that matter, energy, space and time must (at some level) be understood in relation to each other for matter is where space and time and energy are brought together. In more philosophical terms, one could say that unity (representing energy) and diversity (representing space and time) must be kept together. Some emphasize only the elements of unity and continuity and thus tend to say that REALITY (in capital letters) is, or will be, undifferentiated, timeless, and spaceless. Capra and Zukov claim the support of modern physics for this by concentrating on only those elements of modern physics that emphasize continuity. But the elements of diversity, space, and time must be kept together with those of continuity and unity. Thus, the unity here envisioned is not simple continuity, is not the absorption of all diversities into a universal unity as drops of water are absorbed into the sea. The unity of the universe (in physical terms) or of reality (in metaphysical terms) must include diversity, space and time. The elements that stand for unity and continuity can only be understood in relation to the elements that stand for diversity. As long as there is any reality that is in any way analogous or continuous with the present world, there will be diversity, space and time. In religious terms, the future will not be timeless and spaceless but will be transformed time and space: not the vanishing of the heavens and the earth but a new heaven and a new earth. St. Paul says that we (and presumably the universe we inhabit) will live eternally as a spiritual body -- not a timeless, spaceless spirit nor a simple continuation of the present form, but a spiritual body. This is a paradoxical concept for spirits and bodies were thought to be in antithetical in Paul's day, but using such a frankly paradoxical term points to the truth that even the eternal future will have bodily, physical (in the sense of the study of physics) elements. No eternal unity can fail to include some form of the diversity represented now by space and time.

As with the future, so with the present. Here and now the universe, in its present form as well as its future destiny, must be understood in categories of unity in diversity. A radical reconceptualizing of the task of scientific explanation is called for. Analysis emphasized diversity and isolation. Matter was to be reduced to individual atoms which could be understood singularly. In the high energy domain, this type of analysis, which has powered the scientific enterprise for two hundred years, is breaking down. Particles can no longer be understood only as isolated entities but also as points along a process of transformation. Matter can no longer be described fully as discrete bits but rather by recognizing its context in space and time. Along with the logic, language, and procedures of <u>analysis</u>, we need new logic, language and procedures of <u>synthesis</u>.

Science is at the turning point. Analysis has been exceedingly fruitful and cannot be abandoned lightly. It is almost impossible for any of us, so deeply are we heirs to this tradition, to imagine understanding something unless we have broken it down into its parts. Yet such an approach is no longer adequate by itself in the physics of high-energies and relativity theories. Whereas analysis broke things down, synthesis builds them back up until the universe as a whole is the single object of study. Whereas analysis concentrated on bits of things, synthesis concentrates on the <u>relations</u> between things. Before one only understood when one had seen all the parts; now only one understands when one has seen the whole. I am in no position to follow Bohm in speculating on what a new view of scientific explanation based on synthesis will look like, nor what form its quantitative dimensions can take. Nor am I suggesting that analysis be abandoned. However, a new conceptualization, a new way of regarding phenomena and the explanation of them is called for and it will be one in which analysis and breaking down is balanced (not replaced) by synthesis and the perception of inter-relations.

Thus, the first point that emerges from modern physics is that reality must be seen as unity that includes diversity, particularity, and the existence of space and time rather than one that is homogenized, absorbing, and undifferentiated.

Second, matter is always being created and destroyed -- transformed into energy and back again -- according to certain symmetries of natural laws. The creation of the universe is not simply the creation of something called matter-energy for the universe has the form it does because of these conservation principles. Discussions of divine creativity often sound like God's creative act was simply bringing the whole cosmic system into being at one point in time. Such accounts tend towards Deism. In fact, the creation of the universe is not only the emergence of matter, or even energy, but also of the basic symmetries by which energy and matter take form. God's creative act is primarily the creation of those forms and laws that continually shape energy into the structures of our universe. Divine creation is not (as in Deism) something that separates God from nature but something that binds him to it. Nor is creation something that happened just once upon a time but is rather something that continues, at least in an analogous way, to happen every second as matter continues to come into being according to these forms. When God created, he did not magically bring a new substance into being out of nothing but rather generated certain structures, making the universe what it is. The coming into being of these symmetries is a better image for the divine creation than the making of clocks, or even the generation of a few primal atoms, for it is these symmetries that make this universe into *this* universe and not some other. Former images for creation emphasized something that only happened once and thus, "creation" tended to separate God from the present system of nature: However, at every instant, the universe continues to have the form that it does because these symmetries are conserved and in this process the scientist sees the operation of the most fundamental principles of nature and the believer sees an analogy for the sustaining creativity of God.

The Body of the Universe

The breakdown of classical science and the rise of modern physics provide resources for a new theology of nature. The physical world is grounded in and arises out of the immaterial divine Spirit; events that make up the physical world are given their form by the free act of God; the universe is a unity in diversity. The terms immanence and transcendence, which have characterized so much modern discussion of God, are shorn of their spatial connotations. God's immanence is the presence of the Spirit within matter; his transcendence is his freedom to give the universe the form that it has (through the imposition of certain symmetries) and to constitute the events of the universe, not in a chaotic or arbitrary way, but as the product of free and careful choice by which one possibility among many is brought to fruition. God is present to his creation but he is not bound by it. By his free and spiritual activity within the world, God is seeking to fashion it into a spiritual body.

In the past, mechanistic determinism answered the question of what holds the events in the universe together. Since the causal chains that formerly bound the universe have snapped under the weight of phenomena too heavy and complex to handle, no new image for the unity of the universe has emerged. Although no such model is necessary in current scientific theory, it is not discontinuous with current views to perceive the universe as bound together by the presence within it of a freely-acting divine Spirit, pervading the physical reality, constituting the connections between events, giving rise to the matter we perceive. "In him all things were created...all things were created through him and for him...in him all things hold together."

This essay demonstrates that compartmentalized theologies and secular sciences are historical anomalies; for most of mankind's history a mutually enriching relationship has existed between what today we call theology and natural science. With the coming of twentieth-century physics, that relationship may flower again for it no longer appears far-fetched for Christians to say that the physical world is the Body of Christ. When Paul describes the cosmos as the Body of Christ, he describes an organism indwelt by the Spirit, taking its form from the sovereignty of its Head, maintaining unity in diversity as one body with many members. Modern science does not prove this to be true, nor would the collapse of modern science prove it false. But in a way unknown in previous scientific thought, modern science provides analogies for conceiving of the Spirit as the origination of matter, for characterizing natural events as the products of free choice, for perceiving the universe as a whole, and for understanding its wholeness as a single body having many parts. And so the pilgrimage of understanding goes on.

BIBLIOGRAPHY OF SOURCES

Chapter I

PRIMARY SOURCES

The Collected Dialogues of Plato, Ed. E. Hamilton and H. Cairns, (new York: Bollingen Foundation) 1963.
The Basic Works of Aristotle, Ed. R. McKeon, (New York: Random House) 1941.
"The Introduction of Alcinous to the Doctrines of Plato", Bohm's Classical Library, Vol. VI, (London: Bell and Daldy) 1870.
The Essential Plotinus, Ed. E. O'Brien (New York: Mentor Books) 1964.
The Philosophy of Plotinus, Ed. J. Katz (New York: Appleton, Century, Crafts) 1950.

SECONDARY SOURCES

Armstrong, A. H., An Introduction to Ancient Philosophy (London: Methuen) 1957.
Armstrong, A. H. and Markus, R. A., Christian Faith and Greek Philosophy (New York: Sheed and Ward) 1960.
Cornford, F. M., Plato's Cosmology (Cambridge: Cambridge University Press) 1937.
Lovejoy, Arthur, The Great Chain of Being (Cambridge: Harvard University Press) 1937.
Norris, Richard, God and World in Early Christian Theology (New York: Seabury Press) 1936.
Ross, David, Aristotle (New York: Barnes and Noble) 1964.
Rist, John, Eros and Psyche (Toronto: University of Toronto Press) 1964.
Rist, John, Plotinus: The Road to Reality (Cambridge: Cambridge University Press) 1967.
Taylor, A. E., Plato: The Man and His Work (New York: Meridian Books) 1963.
Toulmin, Stephen and Goodfield, June, The Architecture of Matter (New York: Harper and Row) 1962.
Toulmin, Stephen and Goodfield, June, Commentary of the Timaeus (Oxford: Oxford University Press) 1928.

Wallis, R. T., <u>NeoPlatonism</u> (New York: Scribners) 1972.

Witt, R. E., <u>Albinus and the History of Middle Platonism</u> (Cambridge: Cambridge University Press) 1937.

CHAPTER II

PRIMARY SOURCES

All primary sources can be found in the <u>Ante-Nicene Fathers</u> and <u>The Nicene and Post-Nicene Fathers</u> (Grand Rapids: W. B. Erdmans) 1965.

SECONDARY SOURCES

Armstrong, A. H., and Markus, R. A., <u>Christian Faith and Greek Philosophy</u>, op. cit.

Danielou, Jean, <u>Origen</u> (New York: Sheed and Ward) 1960.

deFaye, Eugene, <u>Origen and His Work</u> (London: Allen and Unwin) 1926.

Grant, R. M., "Irenaeus and Hellanistic Culture", <u>Harvard Theological Review</u>, 1949.

Harnack, Adolph Von, <u>History of Dogma</u> (New York: Dover) 1960.

Norris, Richard, <u>God and World in Early Christian Theology</u>, op. cit.

Otis, Brooks, "Cappadocian Theology as a Coherent System" (Cambridge: Harvard University Press) <u>Dumbarton Oaks Papers</u> No. 12, 1958.

Rist, J. M., <u>Eros and Psyche</u>, op. cit.

For a further discussion of the development of the doctrine of the Trinity, see James W. Jones, <u>The Spirit and the World</u> (New York: Hawthorn Press) 1975.

CHAPTER III

CLASSICAL ALCHEMY

Eliade, Mircea, <u>The Forge and the Crucible</u> (Chicago: University of Chicago Press) 1978.

Hopkins, A. J., <u>Alchemy, Child of Greek Philosophy</u> (reissued New York: AMS Press) 1967.

Lindsay, Jack, <u>The Origins of Alchemy in Graeco-Roman Egypt</u> (London: Muller) 1970.

ALCHEMY, GENERAL

Burland, C. A., <u>The Arts of the Alchemists</u> (New York: MacMillan) 1968.

Caron, M. and Hutin, S., *The Alchemists* (New York: Grove Press) 1961.
Edinger, Edward, *Ego and Archetype* (Baltimore: Penguin) Chapter 10, 1973.
Jung, C. G., Collected Works, Volume 12, *Psychology and Alchemy* (Princeton: Princeton University Press) 1967.
Jung, C. G., Collected Works, Volume 13, *Alchemical Studies* (Princeton: Princeton University Press) 1967.
Jung, C. G., Collected Works, Volume 14, *Mysterium Conjunctions* (Princeton: Princeton University Press) 1963.
Powell, Neil, *Alchemy, The Ancient Science* (Garden City: Doubleday) 1976.
Taylor, F. S., *The Alchemists* (New York: Shuman) 1949.
Toulmin, S. and Goodfield, J., *The Architecture of Matter*, op. cit., Chapter 6.
Yates, Francis, *The Rosecrucian Enlightenment* (Chicago: University of Chicago Press) 1972.

SEVENTEENTH CENTURY

Dobbs, B. J. T., *The Foundations of Newton's Alchemy* (Cambridge: Cambridge University Press) 1975.
Debus, A. G. and Multhauf, *Alchemy and Chemistry in the Seventeenth Century* (Los Angeles: University of California, William Andrews Clark Memorial Library) 1966.
Wallis, R. T., *Neoplatonism*, "Magic and Alchemy in Neo-Platonism", op. cit.
Westfall, Richard, *Force in Newton's Physics* (New York: American Elsevier) 1971.

CHAPTER IV

THE GROWTH OF MECHANISM

Barbour, Ian, *Issues in Science and Religion* (New York: Harper and Row) 1966.
Burtt, E. A., *The Metaphysical Foundations of Moder Science* (New York: Humanities Press) 1951.
Christianson, G. E., *This Wild Abyss* (New York: The Free Press) 1978.
Dobbs, Betty Jo, *The Foundations of Newton's Alchemy*, op. cit.
Gillispie, C. G., *The Edge of Objectivity* (Princeton: Princeton University Press) 1960.

Kuhn, Thomas, *The Copernicun Revolution* (Cambridge: Harvard University Press) 1957.
McLachlan, H., *Sir Isaac Newton's Theological Manuscripts* (Liverpool: Liverpool Universit Press) 1950.
Toulmin, S. and Goodfield, J., *The Architecture of Matter*, op. cit.
Toulmin, S. and Goodfield, J., *The Fabric of the Heavens* (New York: Harper and Row) 1961.
Westfall, R. S., *Science and Religion in Seventeenth Century England* (New Haven: Yale University Press) 1958.

THE RESPONSE OF THEOLOGY

Barth, Karl, *Dogmatics in Outline* (New York: Harper and Row) 1959.
Barth, Karl, *Church Dogmatics*, Volumes II, III/i (Edinburgh: T & T Clark) 1961.
Barth, Karl, *The Epistle to the Romans* (London: Oxford University Press) 1933.
Barth, Karl, *From Rosseau to Ritschl* (London: SCM Press) 1959.
Dillenberger, John, *Protestant Thought and Natural Science* (Garden City: Doubleday) 1960.
Hume, David, *Dialogues Concerning Natural Religion* (New York: Hefner) 1948.
Kant, Immanurel, *Critique of Pure Reason* (New York: Humanities Press) 1950.
Kant, Immanurel, *Religion Within the Limits of Reason Alone* (New York: Harper and Row) 1960.
Lessing, Gotthold, *Lessing's Theological Writings* (Stanford: Stanford University Press) 1967.
Mackintosh, H. R., *Types of Modern Theology* (New York: Scribner's) no date.
Paine, Thomas, *The Age of Reason* (New York: Wiley Company) 1942.
Ritschl, Albrecht, *The Christian Doctrine of Justification and Reconciliation*, 3 volumes (Edinburgh: T & T Clark) 1900.
Schleiermacher, Friedrich, *The Christian Faith*, 2 volumes (New York: Harper and Row) 1963.
Tillich, Paul, *Dynamics of Faith* (New York: Harper and Row) 1957.
Tillich, Paul, *Perspectives on Nineteenth and Twentieth Century Protestant Theology* (New York: Harper and Row) 1967.
Tillich, Paul, *Systematic Theology* Volumes I and III (Chicago: University of Chicago Press) 1951 and 1963.

Tillich, Paul, <u>Theology of Culture</u> (New York: Oxford University Press) 1959.
Toland, John, <u>Christianity Not Mysterious</u> (London) 1718.

THE CONSERVATIVE CRUSADE

Furniss, N. F., <u>The Fundamentalist Controversy</u> (New Haven: Yale University Press) 1954.
White, A. D., <u>A History of the Warfare of Science with Theology</u> (New York: Appleton Company) 1896.

Chapter V

BACKGROUND ON THE DEVELOPMENT OF MODERN SCIENCE

Gamov, George, <u>Biography of Physics</u> (New York: Harper and Row) 1961.
Feinberg, Gerald, <u>What is the World Made of</u> (Garden City: Doubleday) 1977.
Feynman, Richard, <u>The Feynman Lectures in Physics</u>, Volumes 1, 2, and 3. (Reading: Addison-Wesley) 1963.
Hesse, Mary, <u>Forces and Fields</u> (Westport: Greenwood Press) 1970.
Heisenberg, Werner, <u>Physics and Philosophy</u> (New York: Harper and Row) 1962.
Toulmin, Stephen and Goodfield, June, <u>Architecture of Matter</u>, op. cit.

Chapter VI

NEO-ORTHODOX POSITION

Dillenberger, John, <u>Protestant Thought and Natural Science</u>, op. cit.
Tillich, Paul, <u>Dynamics of Faith</u>, op. cit.
Tillich, Paul, <u>Systematic Theology</u>, Volume I, op. cit.

METAPHYSICAL IDEALISM IN MODERN SCIENCE

Heisenberg, Werner, <u>Physics and Philosophy</u>, op. cit.
Heisenberg, Werner, <u>Physics and Beyond</u> (New York: Harper and Row) 1972.
Heisenberg, Werner, "The Nature of Elementary Particles", <u>Physics Today</u> (1976).
Schroedinger, Erwin, <u>What is Life and Mind and Matter</u> (Cambridge: Cambridge University Press) 1969.
Schroedinger, Erwin, <u>Nature and the Greeks</u> (Cambridge: Cambridge University Press) 1954.

Jeans, James, <u>Physics and Philosophy</u> (Ann Arbor: University of Michigan Press) 1958.
Jeans, James, <u>The Mysterious Universe</u> (Cambridge: Cambridge University Press) 1930.

THE WORK OF DAVID BOHM

Bohm, David, <u>Causality and Chance in Modern Physics</u> (Philadelphia: University of Pensylvania Press) 1971.
Bohm, David, "Quantum Mecganics as an Indication of a New Order in Physics" Parts A and B, <u>Foundations of Physics</u>, 1975.
Bohm, David, "On the Intuitive Understanding of Nonlocality as Implied by Quantum Theory", <u>Foundations of Physics</u>, 1975.
Bohm, David, "Fragmentation and Wholeness" (New York: Humanities Press) Van Leer Jerusalem Foundation Series, 1973.
Bohm, David, "Holography and a New Order in Physics", unpublished paper, offprint, no date.
Bohm, David, "The Implicate or Enfolded Order -- A New Order for Physics" unpublihed paper from Birkbeck College, University of London, 1975.

CONTROVERSY SURROUNDING BOHM'S WORK

Bastin, Ted, <u>Quantum Theory and Beyond</u> (Cambridge: Cambridge University Press) 1971.
Bohm, D. et. al., <u>Quanta and Reality</u>, Published by the American Research Council, 1962.
Korner, S., <u>Observation and Interpretation</u> (London: Butterworth) 1957.
Toulmin, Stephen, <u>Physical Reality</u> (New York: Harper and Row) 1970.

GEOFFREY CHEW AND BOOTSTRAP THEORIES

Chew, Geoffrey, "Crisis in the Elementary Particle Concept" (Berkeley: University of California Radiation Laboratory) 1967.
Chew, Geoffrey, " Hadron Boot-Strap: Triumph or Frustration", <u>Physics Today</u>, 1970.
Heisenberg, Werner, "The Nature of Elementary Particles", op. cit.
Plus...Capra's work cited below.

MODERN PHYSICS AND EASTERN THOUGHT

Capra, Fritjof, <u>The Tao of Physics</u> (Boulder: Shambhala) 1975.

Postle, Denis, <u>The Fabric of the Universe</u> (New York: Crown) 1976.
Zukav, Gary, <u>The Dancing Wu Li Masters</u> (New York: William Morrow) 1979.

SYSTEMS THEORY

Von Bertalanffy, L., <u>General Systems Theory</u> (New York: Bragiller) 1968.
Gray, W. et. al., <u>General Systems Theory and Psychiatry</u> (Boston: Little Brown) 1969.
Beavers, W. P., <u>Psychotherapy and Growth</u> (New York: Brunnermazel) 1977.

CHAPTER VII

Bohm, David, <u>Causality and Chance in Modern Physics</u>, op. cit.
Jones, James, <u>The Texture of Knowledge: An Essay on Religion and Science</u>, (Washington: University Press of America, 1981).
Monod, Jacques, <u>Chance and Necessity</u> (New York: Vintage Books) 1972.

INDEX

Albinus, see Middle-Platonism
Alchemy, 33-49
Aquinas, Thomas, 40, 50, 54
Aristotle, 3-6, 9, 33, 43, 50
Astrology, 34-35, 43, 52
Augustine, 29
Bacon, Francis, 46, 59
Barth, Karl, 75-77
Bohm, David, 105-107, 120-126
Boyle, Robert, 47, 57-58, 61
Brahe, Tycho, 51
Cappadocian Fathers (Gregory, Gregory, & Basil), 30-32
Capra, Fritjof, 107-114, 129
Conservation laws or symmetries, 103, 110-113, 126-131
Copernicus, Nicholas and Copernican astronomy, 50-54
DeBroglie, Louis, 83
Deism, 63-67, 117
Descartes, Rene, 55-57
Determinism, philosophy of, 51-63, 91-97, 120-126
Dillenberger, John, 99-102
Einstein, Albert, 82-83, 88, 127
Fundamentalist movement, 80-81
Galilio, 53-55
General systems theory, 111-114, 126-133
Gnosticism, 15, 20-23
Heisenberg, Werner, 84, 91-97, 103-104, 120
Hume, David, 67
Immanence of God, see spirit and matter
Indeterminacy, 91-97, 120-127
Irenaeus, 20-23
Jean, James, 105, 120
John, Gospel of, 18, 29
Justin (martyr), 17-21
Kant, Immanuel, 67-69, 75-76
Kepler, Johannes, 51-53, 66
Laplace, 91
Lessing, Gotthold, 65
Logos, 18-20, 22-23, 27-28, 29-32, 44, 120, 131-132
Matter and materialism, 61-63, 85-89, 118-120, 126-132
Matter and energy, 62-62, 84-85, 87-89, 126-131
Matter and spirit, see spirit and matter
Maxwell, James C., 62-63
Mechanism, philosophy of, 51-63, 95-97
Monod, Jacques, 125-126
Neo-Platonism, see Plotinus
Newton, Issac, 47-48, 58-61
Origen, 24-28, 30, 45, 78
Paine, Thomas, 65-66

Plank, Max, 82
Plato, 1-3, 8-9, 11, 15, 16, 29, 103-104
Plotinus and Neo-Platonism, 11-16, 24, 29, 43
Postle, Denis, 107
Ptolemy of Alexandria and Ptolemaic astronomy, 49-50
Quantum theory, early history of, 82-88, 91-95
Quantum theory, Bohm's criticism of, 105-107, 120-122
Ritschl, Albrecht, 69-70
Schleiermacher, Friedrich, 70-74
Schroedinger, Erwin, 104-105, 117, 120
Soul of the world, 2-3, 5-7, 10, 14-15, 103-104
Soul, human, 3, 14, 25-26
Spirit and Matter, 6-7, 10, 13-15, 21, 24, 26-28,
            31-32, 41-45, 60, 89-90, 118-120,
            126-132
Stoicism, 6-7, 23-24, 32
Systems theory, 111-114, 126-133
Tertullian, 23-24, 30
Thomson, J. J., 82
Tillich, Paul, 77-79, 98-99, 101-102
Timaeus, 1-3, 6, 8
Tindal, Matthew, 64-65
Toland, John, 64
Transcendence of God, 5, 9-10, 12-13, 17-23, 26-27,
            30-32, 55, 66-70, 76, 117-120
Trinity, doctrine of, 28-32
Via Negativa in physics and theology, 90, 118-119
Zukav, Gary, 107-114